# THE COMPLETE T
## OF
## LORD KRISHNA

# BHAGAVAD GITA
# AND
# UDDHAVA GITA

## MIKE NACH

THE COMPLETE TEACHINGS OF LORD KRISHNA-BHAGAVAD GITA AND UDDHAVA GITA

Printed in the United States of America

Copyright © 2016 Mike Nach

**All rights reserved.** No part of this book may be reproduced in whole or in part without written permission from the author, except by reviewers who may quote brief excerpts in connection with a review in a newspaper, magazine, or electronic publication; nor may any part of the book be reproduced, stored in a retrieval system, or transmitted in any form by means electronic, mechanical, photocopying, recording, or other, without written permission from the author.

ISBN-13: 978-1533355768

ISBN-10: 1533355762

KDP LINK: https://www.amazon.com/dp/B01FV75BZK

## Table of Contents

Disclaimer ............................................................................. 1
Lord Krishna ........................................................................ 3
Bhagavad Gita ..................................................................... 9
The King and the Psychic .................................................. 11
Arjuna's Dilemma .............................................................. 14
Game of Life ...................................................................... 16
Equanimity in Actions ....................................................... 27
The Secret .......................................................................... 32
Desirelessness .................................................................... 38
How to Meditate ................................................................ 40
The Favorite Devotee ........................................................ 47
Attaining the Universal Consciousness ............................. 51
The Way to Salvation ........................................................ 56
Divine Powers .................................................................... 59
The Cosmic Form .............................................................. 63
Nature, the Enjoyer and Consciousness ............................ 68
The Three Modes of Nature .............................................. 71
The Topsy-Turvy Banyan Tree ......................................... 74
Divine and Demonic Beings .............................................. 77
The Divisions of Faith ....................................................... 80
Renunciation, Knowledge, Work, Workers, Happiness ... 85
Lessons from the Bhagavad Gita ....................................... 92
Uddhava Gita ..................................................................... 97
Lord Krishna and Uddhava ................................................ 99
Uddhava Pleads with Lord Krishna ................................. 104
The Illusory Universe ...................................................... 106

| | |
|---|---|
| The King and the Young Man | 109 |
| The 25 Teachers | 111 |
| Game of Life | 127 |
| The Lord Instructs Brahma | 130 |
| Task of a Devotee | 133 |
| Being Detached | 136 |
| The Tree of Life | 139 |
| Different Gurus, Different Philosophies | 142 |
| The Ancient Yoga Meditational Technique | 146 |
| Earthly Form of Lord Krishna | 150 |
| Transcendental Form of Lord Vishnu | 151 |
| The Mystic Powers | 152 |
| Awakening the Powers | 156 |
| Power 1- Contraction | 158 |
| Power 2- Expansion | 159 |
| Power 3- Lightness | 160 |
| Power 4- Becoming Heavy | 161 |
| Power 5- Manifestation | 162 |
| Power 6- Remote Sensing | 163 |
| Power 7- Lordship | 164 |
| Power 8- Controlling Living Beings | 165 |
| Power 9- Control Body Functions | 166 |
| Power 10- Clairaudience | 167 |
| Power 11- Remote Viewing | 168 |
| Power 12- Astral Travelling | 169 |
| Power 13- Shape Shifting | 170 |
| Power 14- Psychically Enter Another Body | 171 |

Power15- Choosing Time of Death .................................................172
Power 16- Extraterrestrial Contacts .................................................173
Power 17- Intent ..............................................................................174
Power 18- The Power of the Spoken Word ....................................175
Power 19- Precognition and Postcognition .....................................176
Power 20- Physical Tolerance .........................................................177
Power 21- Telepathy ........................................................................178
Power 22- Immunity ........................................................................179
Power 23- Invincibility ....................................................................180
Divine Attributes .............................................................................181
Bheeshma Teaches Self-Realization ...............................................185
Q & A Session .................................................................................188
Path of Devotion .............................................................................194
Miser Who Became a Tramp ..........................................................199
Folly of King Puruvara ...................................................................208
The Soul and the Body ...................................................................213
Bhakti Yoga ....................................................................................216
Samkhya Philosophy ......................................................................221
The Philosopher's Score .................................................................225
The Three Modes of Nature ............................................................230
Deity Worship .................................................................................238
Uddhava Bids Farewell to the Lord ................................................248
Lord Krishna Ascends to Vaikuntha ...............................................250
Thank You! ......................................................................................255
My Other Books! ............................................................................257

# Disclaimer

The author and publisher have used their best efforts in preparing this book. Every effort has been made to accurately represent the techniques mentioned in this book, and their potential. Your level of success in attaining the results claimed in this book depends on the instructions / precautions followed and the time you devote to the techniques and ideas given.

Since these factors differ according to individuals, we cannot guarantee your success. Nor are we responsible for any of your actions. Consulting a competent professional is advisable.

The author and publisher shall in no event be held liable to any party for any direct, indirect, punitive, special, psychological, incidental or other consequential damages arising, directly or indirectly, from any use of this material, which is provided "as is", and without warranties.

If you wish to apply the ideas contained in this book, you are taking full responsibility for your action.

# Lord Krishna

**Lord Krishna** is universally considered to be an Avatar – a direct descent of **Lord Vishnu**.

According to Hindu mythology, Krishna was born in prison to **Devaki** and **Vasudeva**. They had been imprisoned by the tyrant **King Kamsa** who ruled **Mathura** after deposing his father **King Ugrasena**. Devaki was the sister of Kamsa who was seeking to kill Krishna. It had been foretold that Kamsa would be killed by Devaki's eighth child. To play safe, Kamsa had ordered all Devaki's offspring's to be killed, as and when they were born. Lord Krishna, the eighth child, who was destined to kill Kamsa and bring about a new order on Earth, could not be killed. He was smuggled out of prison, by divine forces, to be raised by his foster parents **Nanda** and **Yasoda** in **Gokula**. Nanda was a chief in the local cattle-farming community.

Krishna was a mischievous child, who enjoyed playing pranks and having fun. He also performed many miracles to save his people from dangers like lifting the **Govardhana** hill to protect the villagers against the thunderbolts hurled by the king of the demigods, Indra. He, also, killed many demons deputed by Kamsa to kill him.

As a young adult, Lord Krishna played the role of a divine lover playing the flute for his beloved gopis or female devotees. Of these **Radha** was his greatest devotee. He loved playing pranks with his female devotees. However, his love for his devotees was totally spiritual. The gopis knew this and they felt totally safe with him. It was pure love! Lord Krishna had many wives. His chief consort was **Rukmini.** She was the incarnation of Lord Vishnu's wife, **Laxmi**, the Goddess of Wealth. Many writers have construed Lord Krishna as a playboy God but that was not the case. He loved and cared for all his devotees, male or female, equally. It was divine, spiritual and not physical bonding.

On his return to Mathura, Lord Krishna killed Kamsa and reinstated Ugrasena as King of Mathura. In due course, Lord Krishna befriended the Pandava Prince, **Arjuna**, who was also his paternal cousin. Lord Krishna became a counsel and friend to Arjuna.

Who were the Pandavas? Let's check out the **Mahabharata**.

The Mahabharata is an ancient Indian epic which depicts the dynastic struggle between two groups of paternal first cousins of an Indo-Aryan clan, Kuru.

The two groups, the **Kauravas** and the **Pandavas**, are in constant conflict with each other for the throne of **Hastinapura**.

The five sons of the deceased King Pandu are the Pandavas and the one hundred sons (and one daughter) of the blind **King Dhritarashtra (King D),** the Kauravas. Although the Kauravas are the senior branch of the family, **Duryodhana**, the eldest Kaurava, is younger than **Yudhisthira**, the eldest Pandava. Both Duryodhana and Yudhisthira claim to be first in line to inherit the throne. Lord Krishna tries to mediate a peace settlement between the warring clans, but, to no avail. War was inevitable.

The conflict between the Kauravas and the Pandavas culminates in the great battle of Kurukshetra (Kuru's field). The Kurukshetra War is believed to have taken place in 10th century BCE or 950 BCE, according to archeological evidence.

Vast armies from all over the Indian (Bharat) subcontinent fought alongside the two rivals. Krishna out of affection for his cousin and devotee had agreed to drive his chariot. But, Arjuna, who was one of the foremost archers of the age, is filled with doubts and does not want to fight the enemies who comprise of his relatives, teachers and friends.

He turns to Krishna for solace. Krishna responds by explaining to Arjuna his duties as a warrior and prince, elaborating on a variety of philosophical concepts.

Lord Krishna describes the science of self-realization and how to establish a relationship with God. There's a message in the Bhagavad Gita for everyone.

It teaches us how to face and solve the eternal problems facing mankind- birth, death, pain, suffering, fear, bondage, love and hate. It explains how to reach a state of perfect mental peace, inner stability and complete freedom from grief, fear and anxiety.

Arjuna is enlightened and agrees to fight the war. With the Lord's help, the Pandavas emerge as the reluctant winners in the eighteen day war. The eldest Pandava, Yudhisthira, is crowned the king of Hastinapura. After the battle, Lord Krishna visits Duryodhana's mother, **Gandhari**, to offer his condolences. In a fit of rage and sorrow, Gandhari curses Krishna that just as the Kuru dynasty had ended fighting with each other, likewise, after thirty years, the Yadava clan would end fighting and killing each other.

Gandhari felt that Lord Krishna was responsible for all the bloodshed.

She cursed that Krishna would also die a disgusting death in the forest just like her eldest son, Duryodhana had.

After Yudhisthira's coronation, the erstwhile King Dhritarashtra and his wife Gandhari, accompanied by the Pandava's mother, **Kunti**, retire to the forest where they perish in a forest fire.

Lord Krishna accepts Gandhari's curse and returns to his kingdom, **Dwaraka**. For thirty years, Dwaraka is a realm of peace and happiness. Soon, the D-day arrived.

The destruction of Lord Krishna's clan, the **Yadavas**, was imminent. The Yadavas had gotten very arrogant and if they were unchecked they would have destroyed civilization. Lord Krishna assembles the Yadava nobles and advises them to take their men to a place called Prabhasa and perform rituals for the benefit of the clan. This strategy would turn out to be the starting point for the Yadavas' annihilation.

Lord Krishna's friend and devotee, Uddhava, overheard the conversation and he was totally scared. He could not figure out why Lord Krishna had assembled the Yadavas and asked them to go to Prabhasa. He wondered why he was not asked to accompany the Yadava men. He feared for his safety, after his master's departure. He spills out his fears before the Lord. The Lord assuages his fears.

Uddhava then requests for spiritual guidance.

The Lord responds by discussing the Game of Life, self-realization, the awesome yoga technique for merging with the Supreme, the mystic powers, the mysteries of creation and the vagaries of the mind. Uddhava becomes spiritually enlightened and brave after listening to the Lord's words.

Thus, the Uddhava Gita is the farewell message of Lord Krishna before he departed to Vaikuntha.

**What's the difference between the Bhagavad Gita and the Uddhava Gita?**

In the Bhagavad Gita, Lord Krishna explains to Arjuna his duties as a warrior and prince and elaborates on different Yogic and Vedantic philosophies, whereas in Uddhava Gita, Lord Krishna explains to his friend and devotee, Uddhava, about spirituality, religion, code of conduct for various classes of society and stages of life, supremacy of devotion, different paths to enlightenment, mind as a root cause of all miseries and many other similar topics.

*You will gain a lot of spiritual wisdom after reading this book. This book will blow your mind!*

# Bhagavad Gita

# The King and the Psychic

**Sanjaya**, who was Dhritarashtra's (King D) advisor and charioteer, played a very important role during the war. Sanjaya, who had the gift of remote-viewing, gave a blow-by-blow account of the war to Dhritarashtra.

The Bhagavad Gita forms a part of the narrative. The entire Bhagavad Gita (Song of God) is Sanjaya's recital to Dhritarashtra of the spiritual dialogue between Lord Krishna and the Pandava prince Arjuna.

Let's start-

King D spoke out aloud, "Sanjaya! I'm anxious to know what's happening on the battlefield. Please activate your remote sensing abilities and give me a blow-by-blow account of the situation."

Sanjaya answered, "Yes, Majesty! I'm now focusing my gaze upon the wall in front of us. Lo! I see the battlefield clearly."

King D (excited) exclaimed, "Awesome! Tell me what you see."

Sanjaya spoke, "I see your son, Duryodhana, checking out the battle formation of the Pandavas army alongside his teacher, **Drona**. He is inquiring, "O, guru! I see hordes of great warriors assembled on the opposite side. They are all equipped with various weapons and well versed in battle tactics. We, too, are strong. The invincible Grandsire, **Bheeshma**, is our commander-in-chief. So, I bet, there's nothing to fear. I pray that you will support him throughout the battle." Drona nods his assent.

King D (smiled) and said, "I'm sure, with Grandsire and Drona on our side, there's nothing to fear. Please go on, Sanjaya!"

Sanjaya continued, "The revered Grandsire blew his conch triumphantly. Its sound is like the roar of a lion bringing shivers into the enemy camp. Now, the other allies of the Kuru clan are also creating a din with their conches, drums and cymbals. The noise is deafening."

King D hollered with glee, "I hope the Pandavas figure out what they are in for. How are they reacting to our war cry?"

Sanjaya answered, "On the Pandavas side, Lord Krishna and Arjuna, standing on a great swift chariot, have blown their conches in reply. The various kings have followed suit. They are no less on the decibels front.The uproar has filled everyone's hearts with fear. My gaze is now directed towards Arjuna. He is talking to Lord Krishna who is driving his chariot.

O, King! I sense some totally unexpected event is about to happen soon."

King D (scornful) blurts out, "Krishna is a wily politician! I'm wary of him. He's capable of turning the tables on us. So, focus your attention on these two and check out what these two are discussing."

Sanjaya answered, "Sure, my lord!"

## Arjuna's Dilemma

Arjuna, surveying the battlefield formation requested Lord Krishna, "Dear Krishna, let's check out our enemies' formation. Would you please drive our chariot between the two armies?"

Krishna answered, "Sure. Let's go."

Arjuna (totally confused) said, "But where's the time to do all this? The war bugles and conches have already been sounded. The battle is about to commence soon."

Krishna (with a gleam in his eye) answered, "Check this out."

(So saying, Krishna waved his hand over the battlefield. There was deathly silence. Everybody except Lord Krishna, Arjuna and their horses seemed frozen. Arjuna was awestruck. The mystics believed Krishna was the incarnation of the Supreme Lord Vishnu while his critics thought of him as a master illusionist. Was this one of his illusory tricks?

It appeared as if time had stood still. Krishna then directed their chariot towards the "frozen" Kaurava side. Arjuna observed the formation and noticed that his enemies consisted of his cousins, relatives, teachers and former friends now turned foes. On seeing this, he was flustered.)

Arjuna groaned, "O, God! Are we going to fight these warriors? They are our relatives, teachers and friends. I'm sweaty and my bow is slipping from my hand. My mind is reeling. I see only misfortune ahead. What good is going to come out of this horrid war? Why are we fighting this bloody war for a kingdom?"

Krishna spoke, "That's reality, dear Arjuna."

Arjuna said, "I've had enough Lord. I'm losing my nerve. I don't want to commit the sin of killing my relatives and innocent people. How can I be happy with this? Isn't it true? Those who destroy family traditions go to hell, don't they? I guess I am done with this fighting. I quit."

# Game of Life

Sanjaya spoke, "On seeing Arjuna's forlorn expression, Lord Krishna tried to console him. Let me narrate their conversation."

Krishna said, "O, Arjuna, dear friend! What's wrong with you? Why are you backing out at the last minute? Aren't you a warrior defending your clan? Wake up! Get ready to fight!"

Arjuna answered, "O, Lord! Are you kidding me? How do you expect me to attack my grandfather and my guru? I am what I am because of them. Let's not forget that. No way, I'm going to fight them. What if I succeed in killing them? I don't want their blood on my hands. I hate my treacherous cousins but killing them is a strict no. I'm terribly confused."

Krishna interrupted, "Steady, brother, steady."

Arjuna continued, "No, Krishna! It's impossible to remain calm under such circumstances. Please help me.

My mind's reeling. You're full of wisdom. Please tell me what my duties are and what should I do now?"

Krishna answered, "I get it. You are losing it. But, why are you lamenting for the undesirables? A wise person does not feel sorry for the living or the dead. Do you need to know the **Game of Life**? Okay, here goes. There was never a time when you or I or any of the assembled warriors did not exist. We will certainly exist in the future, also."

Arjuna blurted, "Huh?"

Krishna smiled and said, "Remember what the gurus taught us in school? No? Well! Listen. There's an immortal soul residing within each of our bodies.

It experiences the various stages of the body like birth, childhood, adulthood, old age and death. Once it completes a life cycle, it leaves its present body and goes on to reside in a new body. This goes on and on throughout eternity. This cycle is called "**Reincarnation**" or the "**Game of Life.**"

Arjuna said, "I'm piqued. Carry on."

Krishna spoke, "Joy, sorrow, heat, cold are all temporary experiences arising out of contact with sense objects. We must strive to control these feelings. A wise person who's aware of his or her true identity and not perturbed by these sense perceptions is freed from the miserable conditions which all souls find themselves trapped in. The soul residing in our bodies is imperishable and can never be destroyed. It is a part of **Brahman** or the **Universal Consciousness**. Thus, it's only our physical bodies that can be destroyed.

So, dear Arjuna, gather your wits and fight your enemies. Only fools think that it's the soul that's destroyed. I will again reiterate this- the soul neither destroys nor can be destroyed. The soul has neither birth nor death. It has neither a beginning nor an end."

Arjuna said, "I am totally confused. If it's not possible to slay the immortal and indestructible soul, then who are we killing?"

Krishna answered, "The physical bodies are like garments for the soul. Just as we discard old garments and wear new ones, the soul discards worn out bodies and accepts new ones. I'm going to say this often. The soul cannot be divided, burned, dissolved or desiccated. It is eternal, all pervading, unalterable, stable and without a beginning or an end. Only physical bodies get killed.

In this Game of Life, births and deaths are unavoidable. We don't need to be worried about this unassailable fact. Those who die are soon reborn. So, why cry over the Self that is manifest in every being and is eternal and indestructible."

Arjuna was totally captivated.

Krishna continued, "You're a warrior and your duty therefore is to fight. A good warrior fights for justice or duty (**dharma**). If you do not fight, you are foregoing your duties as a warrior. People are going to call you a coward and traitor. Can you live with that?"

Arjuna answered, "I guess not."

Krishna said, "So, warrior! Treat joy and sorrow; victory and defeat; gain and loss with equanimity and be ready for battle. You're not committing any sin by your actions."

Arjuna asked, "Does this knowledge give us a license to kill?"

Krishna answered, "You're a warrior about to fight a horrible war. A warrior's duty is to fight for his kingdom and slay his enemies. Killing innocent citizens is off limits!

**I'm also going to shout this out for all mankind to hear:** This killing rule is not applicable to individuals in normal times and situations. Take the help of law enforcement authorities, to deal with your situation. Every soul is playing a role within their bodies.

You've no right to terminate any soul's role by killing the body in which it resides. If you do, you'll be punished in this life and the subsequent ones.

So, no senseless killings are allowed in the Game of Life. Please follow the laws of the state in which you reside."

Arjuna agreed, "That makes sense."

Krishna spoke, "I'm now going to tell you some nuggets which will free you from the bondage that results from your **karma** or actions. Individuals born in this world have many duties or dharma to perform during their lifetimes. It is imperative we should perform our prescribed duties. If you do not do so, you'll be easily distracted.

Then there are some people who give undue importance to the religious scriptures. Their interpretation of the scriptures leaves much to be desired. These false prophets try to impose their half-baked knowledge on the masses with the sole intention of preying on their fears and amassing wealth. They are deluded into thinking that by just following the rituals and sermons they will attain heaven after death or be born in very fortunate circumstances.

Using religion in this way gives it a very bad name."

Arjuna nodded his head in agreement.

Krishna continued, "Never fall prey to such religious bigotries. Just as a reservoir is of little use when the whole countryside is flooded, scriptures are of little use to the illumined man or woman, who sees the Lord everywhere."

Arjuna agreed, "Absolutely!"

Krishna spoke, "Having become a warrior, it is imperative that you act like a warrior. Do not be inactive or hanker for any benefits resulting from your actions. Follow your duties without any hope of enjoying the fruits of your actions."

Arjuna inquired, "No benefits? It does not make sense."

Krishna answered, "Let me explain. The essence of **yoga** is to fix your mind to do your assigned duty without thinking of getting any benefits from it.

If you follow this adage, you'll get rid of good and bad karma that will stick to you, otherwise.

Do not be deluded like the millions on this planet. If you renounce the fruits of your action, you'll become peaceful. You'll realize how insanely stupid have some of the gurus been to preach otherwise. If you're **desireless** and not confused by pseudo-religious nonsense, you'll be truly peaceful and powerful."

Arjuna said, "O, Lord! Tell me about those who have become desireless. How do they behave? How do they interact with other people?"

Krishna answered, "A "desireless" person is one who has renounced all desires born of the mind. Such individuals are neither affected by happiness or suffering. He who is free from desires, passions, fear and anger is said to be a **desireless** or **tranquil** person.

If you're able to control your senses and keep away from temptation, you'll become a **steady** person."

Arjuna spoke, "Is it enough if I turn away from sense objects to avoid being tempted by them?"

Krishna answered, "It's not enough. Turning away from sense objects will not help if the desire for such objects linger.

You need to cut yourself totally from the taste of such objects. I agree that it's a difficult act to follow. The physical senses are so empowering that they can dissuade the hardiest of men."

Arjuna inquired, "Then how do I become a steady person?"

Krishna spoke, "In order to attain steady wisdom, you need to restrain your senses and focus your mind and being on the **Supreme Soul** or the **Universal Consciousness**. Try to restrain your thoughts about sense objects, however tempting they may be, to avoid being lured by them.

Attachment breeds desire and desire gives rise to frustration and frustration leads to delusions.

If you're deluded, you lose your memory and self-control which, in turn, makes you forfeit your power of discrimination. If you lose this ability then you're a lost soul.

A steady person, however, can move among the sense objects without being tempted by them. He remembers his true identity and attains God's grace. If such a person is fixed in this consciousness even at the moment of death he will merge with the Universal Consciousness."

Arjuna asked, "How does one attain this steady state?"

Krishna answered, "Purity of mind will erase all sufferings. If you're disciplined you can attain the steady state. If your mind is steady, you'll be able to meditate easily. Meditation will give you peace and what is happiness without peace?

Do the many rivers entering the ocean disturb its stillness? No! Similarly, the many desires entering the mind of a steady person should not disturb his inner calm. A person who hankers after material desires does not attain peace because he will never be satisfied."

## Equanimity in Actions

Arjuna spoke, "O, Krishna! You have been saying that knowledge of the self is more important than action. Yet, you're goading me to fight. Why this ambiguity? Please explain."

Krishna answered, "Let me explain. If the soul has taken part in the Game of Life then it needs to be active. Abstaining from work will not help it to be free from any karmic reactions. At the same time renunciation helps to attain perfection.

All souls are forced to take part in this Game of Life and therefore no one can refrain from doing something, even for a second. One who tries to control the senses and the sensory organs but is not able to control his mind is suffering from delusions about his self-control. He's just a pretender. On the other side, a soul who is able to control his mind and carries out his earthly work without any desires is the one to be."

Krishna continued, "So, Arjuna, perform your prescribed duty as a warrior. It is certainly better than not working. Think of the worldly activities as a duty to be performed in this world and go about it dispassionately. You'll be free from mental and physical bondages, if you do so."

Arjuna agreed, "I get it, Lord."

Krishna said, "A person who remembers his true self and rejoices in this knowledge remains fully satisfied with his life. He is beyond worldly duties. Such people do not need to depend on any other human being. He ultimately merges with the Universal Consciousness.

Great kings, perform their earthly duties to set an example for their subjects. Even God works to maintain law and order in the universe. If he stops working, then there would be chaos and all laws would be broken."

Arjuna looked at the Lord inquiringly.

Krishna noticed this and answered, "You heard it correctly. Even though no work is prescribed for the Supreme Soul, he has to work to take care of his creation. There is nothing in the three worlds for him to gain, Arjuna, nor is there anything he does not have. The Supreme Soul continues to act, but is not driven by any need of his own.

Most souls perform their duties and hanker after results. Due to ignorance they feel responsible for their actions and become totally unhappy with their existence."

Arjuna inquired, "Shouldn't we try to talk it out with such people about the folly of their actions?"

Krishna spoke, "Try doing that! They will turn a deaf ear. Talking straight is not going to help. A wise man needs to use his guile and carefully chosen words to convince ignorant people not to hanker after results but work without expecting anything for their efforts."

Arjuna agreed, "I totally agree! Lord, tell me this.- What compels a person to commit sinful acts, even unwillingly, as if he has no control over himself?"

Krishna answered, "It's called **lust**. Passion arouses lust; if lustful desires do not get satiated, it turns into anger; anger forces a person to commit horrid crimes in this world.

No one's totally immune from lustful desires. It's best to nip lust in the bud before it totally engulfs its victim.

Act fast. Don't allow lustful thoughts to grow within you."

Arjuna asked, "How do I control my lusty desires?"

Krishna answered, "Our senses are superior to all matter; the mind is higher than the senses; intelligence is still higher than the mind and the soul is superior to all the above.

Thus, one must realize his true identity as the immortal soul, who is superior to everything in this universe, and not allow lust to act as a spoiler."

# The Secret

Krishna continued, "I'm going to repeat this often for the concept to sink in. Every soul has the right to perform its prescribed duty but at the same time it should not expect any fruits for its actions. It should be steadfast in its duty and abandon all attachment to either success or failure. Such a state of mind is called **yoga**.

At the beginning of time I expounded two paths for the realized souls: **jnana yoga**, the contemplative path of spiritual wisdom, and **karma yoga**, the active path of selfless service.

I taught this science of yoga to many advanced souls. They, in turn, imparted this knowledge to their disciples. Thus, successive generations learned about this sacred knowledge. Somewhere, the chain got broken and people soon forgot what yoga was truly about. They identified yoga with breathing techniques and various poses. It's not just mechanical stuff. Yoga is something beyond that.

I'm going to let you into this secret because you're my devotee as well as my friend."

Arjuna exclaimed, "Lord! Are you kidding me? You're not much older than me. How do you claim to have taught yoga to people who lived centuries ago?"

Krishna (bemused) answered, "Haven't I told you that we are all immortal souls inhabiting our physical bodies to play this never ending Game of Life?

However, there's a difference between you and me.

I remember all my previous births clearly, while you don't. I know everything which has happened in the past, all that is happening in the present and all things that are yet to come about."

Krishna continued, "I represent the Universal Consciousness. I'm the Super Soul among souls. I'm now in this human form to teach sinners a lesson.

Whenever there is a serious law and order situation, I manifest myself as a human or non-human (**avatar**) to save innocent people from tyrannical conditions on earth. I have assumed various forms, in every age, to protect the good, to destroy evil, and to reestablish law and order.

Believe this. You'll be free from this Game of Life and merge with the Universal Consciousness."

Arjuna agreed, "I believe you, Lord!"

Krishna spoke, "Since the dawn of time, men have been worshipping superior beings, from the heavenly planets, as gods. These demigods, in order to spread the myth, help those who steadfastly believe in them by granting them special favors.

A wise soul knows that the material gains received from such gods are temporary. Comes in through one door and goes out through the other! Thus, he is not allured by such gods and their temporary benefits.

They perform their duties without expecting anything in return and are totally satisfied with their way of life."

Arjuna inquired, "You've been talking about action and inaction. Does action mean movement and inaction mean sitting still? These concepts are not sinking in. Could you please throw some light?"

Krishna answered, "Even the most intelligent amongst men are bewildered in determining what action is and what inaction is. Listen carefully.

A wise person sees inaction in action (an enlightened person knows that action, which is commonly supposed by all to pertain to the Self, does not really belong to the Self, just as motion does not really pertain to the distant mountains which appears, to an observer sitting in a moving vehicle, to move in the opposite direction).

And action in inaction (inaction is but a cessation of bodily and mental activities, and like action it is falsely attributed to the Self and causes the feeling of egoism as expressed in the words "quiet and doing nothing, I sit happy") whilst carrying out his prescribed duties.

A wise person knows instinctively what kind of work to do or avoid, and how to reach a state of calm detachment from his work. He is not perturbed by either success or failure unlike most people. After death, his soul, having understood the secret of the Game of Life, merges with the Universal Consciousness, and lives in eternal bliss."

Arjuna questioned, "What about the individuals who have been leading ascetic lives, meditating in isolation for ages and torturing themselves by sitting in difficult yogic postures?"

Krishna spoke, "Since these souls have sacrificed a lot to understand the divine truth, they are, in their own contorted way, practicing desirelessness.

Such souls, who have become detached to worldly pleasures and results, are fit to merge with the Universal Consciousness and gain salvation."

Arjuna said, "Thank you, Lord! I've figured out **the hidden secret** in the Game of Life. It's this- a soul who has renounced the fruits of his actions and who is situated firmly in the Self becomes liberated and eventually merges with the Universal Consciousness, to live in eternal bliss."

Lord Krishna smiled.

## Desirelessness

Arjuna inquired, "O Krishna, what carries more weight? Renunciation or working without desires?"

Krishna answered, "Both are evenly balanced. However, I will vote for "working without desires" to have the upper hand.

A liberated person is one who neither hankers nor refuses the fruits of his activities. He simply remains detached from the outcome of his work. This attitude gives him a peace of mind."

Arjuna asked, "What about renunciation?"

Krishna spoke, "What's the use of renouncing the world, living the life of a monk, when your mind is filled with dirty thoughts? A person needs to renounce the temptation for worldly desires and learn to control his mind and senses if he wants to be truly liberated.

A person who does not jump with joy when he gets a lucky break or cries when he loses is truly a liberated person. He knows that success or failure are a part of the Game of Life and are associated with the actions of the physical body. The immortal soul is unaffected by the ups and downs since it knows that they are a part of the game.

If you understand this concept, you'll definitely merge with the Universal Consciousness and be free from taking any further part in the Game of Life."

## How to Meditate

Arjuna said, "I've not figured out what yoga is truly about. Would you care to explain?"

Krishna answered, "A person is said to have attained to yoga when he renounces all material desires and does not hanker after worldly pleasures.

The mind is a friend as well as an enemy of the soul. Calmness, gentleness, silence, self-restraint, and purity-these are the disciplines of the mind. If you're able to control your mind, it will be the best of friends but if you let it control you, it will turn out to be your worst enemy."

Arjuna asked, "How do I control the mind?"

Krishna spoke, "Practice meditation.

When meditation is mastered, the mind is steady like the flame of a lamp in a windless place. Those who eat too much or eat too little, who sleep too much or sleep too little, will not succeed in meditation.

But those who control their eating, sleeping, working habits and recreation will find peace through meditation. Meditation is superior to severe asceticism and the path of knowledge. It is also superior to selfless service. Even among those who meditate, the individual who worships me with perfect faith and is completely absorbed in me, is the most firmly established in yoga.

The Self reveals itself when the mind is stilled during meditation. Beholding the Self by means of the Self, a yogi knows the joy and peace of complete accomplishment."

Arjuna inquired, "How do I meditate? Is there a technique?"

Krishna replied, "Yes, there is. Check this out.

- Choose a secluded place which is free from visual and auditory distractions.
- Select a seat that is neither too high nor too low. It should be comfortable to sit on.

- Now you can either sit cross-legged, in the classic yogic pose, or keep your feet firmly on the ground. The choice is yours.
- Hold your body, neck and head erect in a straight line and stare steadily at the tip of your nose.
- Take relaxed breaths and focus your attention on the air flowing in and out of your nostrils. This will help you relax.
- After you become relaxed and your mind has stilled considerably, fix your attention on me.
- Think of me as situated within you and guiding you.
- You'll need to practice this technique continuously to attain perfection.
- You'll eventually be able to control your mind and senses and become connected to the Universal Consciousness.

If you're able to do this, you will become a yogi who has realized the beauty of his Self and lost the desire for worldly pleasures which never get satiated."

Arjuna said, "I'm not sure whether I got the hang of your technique. What if my mind continues to wander about during meditation?"

Krishna answered, "Controlling the mind is an onerous task. Have you ever noticed this? If you seriously desire something or someone then all your attention is focused on the thought of the item or person of your desire. You don't think of anything else. You want to take actions to achieve your goal. It's all about the intensity of one's desires.

Ponder over the miseries of the Game of Life. Do you want to be entangled in this never ending game? No? How do you make that happen? Stay connected with the Supreme Soul to attain eternal bliss.  Make God your ultimate goal in life. Gradually, your mind will stay focused on God.

Does this make sense?"

Arjuna replied, "It's taking time to sink in, Lord. Please tell me about the characteristics of a true yogi."

Krishna said, "A true yogi sees God in all beings and also sees every being as a part of God or the Universal Consciousness. He knows the Universal Consciousness pervades the entire universe and remains blissful with this knowledge.

A true yogi renounces all selfish desires and breaks away from the ego barricade of "I," "me," and "mine" to be united with the Lord. This is the supreme state."

Arjuna interrupted, "Hey, Lord! Forgive me! I pondered about your yogic meditative technique and I'm still harboring some doubts."

"Doubts?"

Arjuna continued, "I'm sorry, Lord, but it does not seem doable for me. I don't think I'll be able to rein in my restless mind with this meditative technique."

Krishna spoke, "I understand that it's difficult to control the restless mind but not impossible. You need to practice diligently and learn how to be detached in your outlook.

Try this- remember you're an immortal soul residing in this perishable body to play a role in the Game of Life.

You're playing this role because your mind has led you to this.

It's the mind which has made you a prisoner and subject to all miseries including births and deaths. Your true nature is to be a part of the Universal Consciousness and be eternally blissful. If you accept this fact then do not allow your mind to control you. Ignore its beguiling thoughts. With constant practice and determination you'll be successful."

Arjuna said, "This makes sense. There's this question which has been bugging me. I know of some individuals who were initially gung-ho about attaining self-realization but later, on finding the going tough, have abandoned their efforts. What's in for them? Are they losers in the Game?"

Krishna answered, "Any soul quitting the path of self-realization midway cannot be termed a loser.

After it quits this body, it is reborn in a family whose members are spiritually inclined. Under such circumstances, the soul subconsciously remembers the incomplete task of its previous birth and endeavors to complete it. It will continue to take further births until its goal is accomplished. Having done so, it merges with the Universal Consciousness and becomes free from the cycle of births and deaths of the Game of Life."

## The Favorite Devotee

Krishna continued, "Earth, water, fire, air, ether, mind, intelligence and false ego comprise the Universal Consciousness' separated material energies. Then there are the souls who are playing the Game of Life and those, realized souls, who are a part of me.

The Universal Consciousness is the creator as well as the destroyer of the Game of Life. He is omnipresent, omnipotent and omniscient. There's not a single place in this universe or beyond where I am not present. I know it's very difficult to comprehend what I'm saying because most souls are deluded by the three modes of nature namely **goodness, passion** and **ignorance**."

Arjuna inquired, "Why have we have traded eternal bliss for miseries? By the way, are you affected by the three modes of nature?"

Krishna smiled, "The Universal Consciousness though a part of the three modes of nature is not controlled by it.

It is the souls of living beings who are ensnared by the modes of nature. They have traded eternal bliss to play roles in the Game of Life."

Arjuna questioned, "How does one cut himself free from the three modes of nature?"

Krishna spoke, "If a soul realizes his true Self and surrenders to the Universal Consciousness, he can easily overcome the three modes of nature and become free."

Arjuna asked, "Tell me about the souls who render devotional service to you."

Krishna replied, "There are four types of individuals who worship God or the Universal Consciousness- the distressed; one who hankers after fame, fortune and success; then there are the inquiring minds and finally the one who hankers to know the absolute truth.

A person who has knowledge of the Self, the Game of Life and the Universal Consciousness is very dear to me.

This person carries out his worldly duties without expectations and his mind is forever concentrated on his true identity and me. He sees see the Lord within every living being. Seeing the same Lord everywhere, he does not harm himself or others. Such a person attains the supreme goal.

The other three types of devotees are also good but the self-realization aspect is missing in them. It's going to take them many births before they realize the absolute truth and return back to me."

Arjuna inquired, "What about the atheists who steadfastly refuse to believe in you?"

Krishna spoke, "These souls will continue to be deluded by material pleasures and sorrows and will never be able to quit the Game of Life. They will be playing miserable roles until they can take it no more and start realizing what they missed all along."

Arjuna persisted, "What's the fate of sinners?"

Krishna answered, "The most sinful of sinners will be able to incinerate all their sins by the fire of spiritual wisdom. Sin cannot touch them if they steadfastly refuse to be deluded by temptations."

## Attaining the Universal Consciousness

Arjuna asked, "Master, what is Brahman? What are fruitive activities? Who are the various gods whom we worship?"

Krishna answered, "The indestructible, transcendental living entity is called Brahman and his eternal nature is called the soul, atman or the Self. Any action carried out by the soul in the physical bodies is called karma or fruitive activities.

There are countless inhabited planets in the universe. Some of the civilizations are very much advanced compared to Earth. I had appointed the best amongst these beings to assist man on the path of evolution and self-discovery. On my bidding, these advanced beings visited Earth and tried to awaken man's inner faculties and development. Man in turn began to worship these beings as gods and prayed for material and spiritual benefits. These beings also love their roles and try to fulfill the wishes of devotees who worship them earnestly.

Since it's difficult to comprehend the Universal Consciousness, wise sages and developed souls have also approved the worship of these demigods. Thus, those who worship the demigods with faith and devotion also worship me, even if they do not observe the usual forms. I am the object of all worship, its enjoyer and Lord."

Arjuna asked, "What if I do not want to play this Game of Life with its myriad pleasures and sorrows? How do I return back to the Universal Consciousness?"

Krishna replied, "Any individual who's done with the Game of Life and wants to live in eternal bliss with me needs to constantly think about me while going about with his worldly duties. Think of the Universal Consciousness as the Super Soul, who is immortal, omnipresent, omniscient and controller of the universe.

Think of him as your **Best Friend Forever (BFF).** Be a detached person!"

Arjuna inquired, "What should a person, who knows death is at his doorstep, do to connect with the Universal Consciousness?"

Krishna said, "A person, who is aware of his impending death, should fix his gaze between the eyebrows and with full faith and devotion remember me, the Supreme Soul, to return back to my fold and live in eternal bliss."

Arjuna questioned, "How do yogis attain salvation?"

Krishna answered, "A yogi or an accomplished person, at the time of his death, stops thinking about all material objects. He focuses his attention on the crown of his head. He starts vibrating the sacred syllable "**OM**" until his soul leaves the body from the top of his head."

Arjuna continued, "What about self-realized devotees?"

Krishna replied, "A devotee who constantly remembers me and knows his true identity merges with me in the Universal Consciousness, after death, to never return to play this Game of Life."

Arjuna spoke, "I've heard astrologers proclaiming that a certain individual died during an auspicious time period and so his soul will go to the heavenly planets to enjoy heavenly pleasures whereas a person who died during an inauspicious period goes to the hellish planets to suffer. Is this true?"

Krishna answered, "Good question! I'll explain to you what are the auspicious and inauspicious periods and their impact on the time of death.

Those souls who are self-realized, leave their bodies during day time; when the sun is burning bright; at an auspicious moment; during the fortnight of the visible moon and when the sun is in the northern hemisphere, never return to play the Game of Life.

The soul who leaves its body at night; during foggy conditions; the moonless fortnight or when the sun is in the southern hemisphere comes back to play the Game of Life."

# The Way to Salvation

Krishna continued, "O, Arjuna, now listen to the most secret wisdom, the knowledge of which will help you attain salvation.

The Universal Consciousness is omnipresent. All matter and energy of the universe are resting in the Universal Consciousness but the Universal Consciousness is not in them. All the created universes undergo a cycle of creation and dissolution. The universe begins as a small dot, expands and after billions of earth years of existence it contracts and gets absorbed within me."

Arjuna spoke, "It's so overwhelming! You also spoke about countless inhabited planets other than earth. Do we get to live there?"

Krishna answered, "As I said earlier, there are countless planets with advanced civilizations (heavenly planets) and those with less developed civilizations (hellish planets).

The inhabitants of the heavenly planets are called the **demigods** and the most advanced planet is called "**Indralok**" or "**Swarga**" or "**Heaven**." Its ruler is **Indra**. These demigods enjoy all sorts of pleasures on their planets and their lifespan is considerable as compared with the human life span.

Human souls who worship the demigods with devotion get to live on these planets and enjoy their hospitality for a long period before they return back to Earth to play the Game of Life. Evil souls who do not believe in me or the demigods go to the hellish planets called "**Patala**," where demons or asuras reside. These souls become slaves of their demonic masters and live a hellish life for a long period before they return to Earth and take birth as losers.

No human soul gets to live forever on these planets. They are just part time visitors."

Arjuna inquired, "So, worshipping the demigods will not give lasting happiness?"

Krishna replied, "You bet! If a soul needs to experience everlasting happiness and bliss they should devote themselves steadfastly to me to be free from the Game of Life.

Always be grateful to the Universal Consciousness for the benefits received by you. Become a righteous person and you'll receive everlasting peace. Think of me as the source of everything and worship me with your mind, body and soul. You'll be with me for eternity!"

## Divine Powers

Arjuna inquired, "You're the Super Soul, the Absolute truth and the Eternal Divine being. You're indiscernible, the unborn, the original and all-pervading divinity. You're a mystery even to the wisest among all souls. Please tell me in detail of your divine powers by which you pervade the universe and abide in them. How do I contemplate you, O blessed Lord?"

Krishna smiled, "Dear Arjuna, what's the need to know all this? I've already talked about myself, and so, I will be brief with my description.

- I am the beginning, middle, and end of creation.
- I am the father and mother of this universe, and its entire support.
- I support the entire cosmos with only a fragment of my being.
- The birth and dissolution of the cosmos itself take place in me. There is nothing that exists

separate from me. The entire universe is suspended from me as my necklace of jewels.

- I am time, the destroyer of all.
- I am the supreme poet, the first cause, the sovereign ruler, subtler than the tiniest particle, the support of all, inconceivable, bright as the sun, beyond darkness.
- All the scriptures lead to me; I am their author and their wisdom.
- I am heat; I give and withhold the rain. I am immortality and I am death; I am what is and what is not.
- I am the taste of pure water and the radiance of the sun, moon and other heavenly bodies.
- I am the sacred word and the sound heard in air, and the courage of human beings.
- I am the ritual and the sacrifice; I am the offering and the fire which consumes it, and the one to whom it is offered.
- I am the sweet fragrance in the earth and the radiance of fire.

- I am the life in every creature and the striving of the spiritual aspirant.
- I enter breathing creatures and dwell within as the life-giving breath. I am the fire in the stomach which digests all food.
- My eternal seed is found in every creature.
- I am the power of discrimination in those who are intelligent, and the glory of the noble. In those who are strong, I am strength, free from passion and selfish attachment.
- I am desire itself, if that desire is in harmony with the purpose of life.
- I am the friend of all creatures, the Lord of the universe, the end of all offerings and all spiritual disciplines.
- I am the sum of all knowledge, the purifier, the syllable Om; I am the sacred scriptures.
- I am the goal of life, the Lord and support of all, the inner witness, the abode of all. I am the only refuge, the one true friend of my believers.

- I am ever present to those who have realized me in every creature. Seeing all life as my manifestation, they are never separated from me."

# The Cosmic Form

Arjuna said, "Thank you, Lord! I'm truly blessed. I'm still curious about one thing."

Krishna asked, "What's that?"

Arjuna replied, "Please forgive my brevity, Lord! I've seen you in this human form but I wish to see you in your cosmic form."

Krishna smiled, "I'm afraid it's impossible to see my cosmic form with your physical eyes. My cosmic form is symbolic. It's just a representation of my activities. I'll need to give you psychic sight to behold my cosmic form."

So saying, Lord Krishna touched Arjuna's eyes.

"Behold, Arjuna, a million divine forms, with an infinite variety of colors and shapes. Behold the gods of the natural world, and many more wonders never revealed before. Behold the entire cosmos turning within my body, and the other things you desire to see."

Sanjaya (in Hastinapura) gasped, "O Majesty, after Prince Arjuna was bestowed with psychic vision, Lord Krishna displayed his Universal form. OMG! This form is beyond description. It's freaking me out.

I see unlimited faces, mouths, eyes, limbs, creatures all morphed into one singular being. The form has worn many dazzling ornaments and dressed in multitude of garments. There's sweet fragrance all around. The luminosity around the figure is as if a million suns are focusing their light on him. Arjuna is shivering in sheer fright and has started praying…"

Krishna spoke, "Satisfied? No mortal has ever seen what you have seen- not by knowledge of the Vedas / sacrifice / charity / rituals or even by severe asceticism!"

Arjuna croaks, "Thank you, Lord, for this incomprehensible divine vision. I've had enough. After seeing this inscrutable form, I'm totally freaked out. Please show your other form as the four armed Lord Vishnu and then revert back to my loving friend Krishna."

Sanjaya narrated, "The Supreme Soul then displayed to Arjuna, his most beautiful four armed "Lord Vishnu" form and finally he became the most beautiful human being –Lord Krishna."

King D cried out, "If the Supreme Lord is on the side of the Pandavas, we're truly lost. Why the heck did I not try to stop this bloody war?"

Sanjaya commented, "Don't fret Majesty! Everything that was to happen has happened.

Did you not hear me telling you that we are immortal souls inhabiting physical bodies and playing a role in the Game of Life? Wait! Let's listen to what Arjuna is saying to Lord Krishna."

Arjuna whispered, "Welcome back, dear Krishna! I'm glad that you are back as Lord Krishna. This human form of yours is very beautiful to behold. I've seen extra-terrestrials watching you enviously from their space vehicles."

Krishna spoke, "Thank you so much for your compliments, Arjuna.

I guess everybody hankers to see my human form since they can relate to it. A true devotee worshipping this form of mine easily attains me after death. He is a **bhakti yogi**."

Arjuna replied, "Lord! What is **bhakti yoga**?"

Krishna answered, "Bhakti yoga is the surest way for the individual soul to realize God because it does not involve difficult yogic practices.

It is simply devotional service to the Supreme Lord or the Universal Consciousness without any aspirations other than pleasing him. A bhakti yogi spends his time with true devotees of the Lord, attends religious sermons delivered by genuine spiritual gurus and spreads the Lord's message."

Arjuna questioned, "What if a person does not want to be a bhakti yogi?"

Krishna answered, "Be a righteous person. Don't be egoistic, lustful and greedy. Do not be perturbed by the ups and downs of life. Think of it as a game and play along.

Be aware of the Lord situated beside you in your physical body. Talk to him and ask for his guidance, direction and clarity in every area of your life. Believe God is there to help you out of any messy situation you'll ever face in this Game of Life. Think of him as the friend of all creatures, the Lord of the universe, the end of all offerings and all spiritual disciplines. You'll attain eternal peace. Also, offer the Lord – the food you eat, the work you do, the help you give and even your suffering. You'll be blessed.

**This is the secret of happiness.**"

Arjuna spoke, "I'm feeling happy, already. What you told me is a game-changer. Thank you very much, Lord."

## Nature, the Enjoyer and Consciousness

Arjuna continued, "O, Krishna, please tell me something about **prakriti** (nature), **purusha** (the enjoyer), the **field** and the **knower of the field**."

Krishna answered, "The physical body is called the field and the one who knows the nature of this body is called the knower of the field. I'm also the knower in all bodies. **Knowledge** means understanding the body and its owner."

Let me explain what the field of activity is and its interactions. The five elements, false ego, intelligence, the unmanifested, the ten senses, the mind, the five sense objects, desire, hatred, happiness, sadness, life symptoms and convictions comprise the field of activity.

Humility, nonviolence, tolerance, patience, cleanliness, persistence, self-restraint, avoidance of sense objects, knowledge of the Self and about the Game of Life, discrimination, devotion to God, living a detached life, knowing what's right and what's wrong, learning about the universal truths- all these are an aggregate called knowledge and anything left out would be ignorance."

Arjuna interrupted, "Knowledge is all encompassing."

Krishna continued, "Let me explain to you what is knowable. The Brahman or the Super Soul or The Universal Consciousness lies beyond the cause and effect of the universe.

The Super Soul exists everywhere. He is the original source of all senses, yet he is without senses. He maintains all living beings but is unattached to anyone. He is beyond everything but also near to all.

The Super Soul lives with the individual soul in all bodies. Haven't you heard the saying, "**God is within us all**?" If you see God in every living being you'll love everybody without discrimination and become a true yogi.

An enlightened person ceases to discriminate between different souls inhabiting different physical bodies. He knows that an immortal soul, residing in every living body, is playing its role in the Game of Life. Most importantly, all these souls have come from a common source-the Universal Consciousness. If you're able to grasp this knowledge, you'll be truly enlightened and attain self-realization."

## The Three Modes of Nature

Arjuna beseeched, "Lord, please tell me something about the three modes of nature."

Krishna answered, "The material nature consists of three modes- **goodness, passion** and **darkness** or **ignorance**. Every living being is affected by these modes.

The mode of goodness is purest amongst the three and it frees one from all sinful reactions. If you follow the goodness route you gain knowledge and positive outlook.

The mode of passion arises out of our unlimited desires and longings. If you follow the road of passion then you get bound to fruitive activities.

Do you know why most living entities are deluded? It's because they travel on the path of ignorance. A deluded person is prone to madness, indolence and sloth.

Let's check out what happens if there is an imbalance in any of the three modes-

If there is goodness all around, there's knowledge and happiness.

If there is an increase in the mode of passion then you get to see great attachment, uncontrolled desires and hankering after sense and material gratification.

And, if there's an excess of the mode of ignorance, you will observe an epidemic of madness, disillusion, sloth and negative conditions all around."

Arjuna inquired, "What happens to an individual, who is attached to any of the three modes, after his death?"

Krishna spoke, "If a "good" person dies, the soul enters the higher planets where it enjoys heavenly delights for a long, long time.

If a "passionate" person dies, his soul takes birth in families sharing similar tendencies.

If an "ignorant" person dies then the soul takes birth amongst the most primitive tribes and families who are ignorant, illiterate and evil."

Arjuna questioned, "Are there souls who are unaffected by the three modes? If so, how do they remain unperturbed? What's their behavior pattern?"

Krishna replied, "I guess you've figured out what I'm going to reply. I've been repeating this fact often in our discussion. It's this- A person who carries out his worldly duties without attachment to results and is aware of his true identity / relation with the Supreme Soul remains unaffected by the three modes of nature. He merges with the Universal Consciousness and attains salvation."

Arjuna spoke, "I guess most souls have different proportions of the three modes within them."

Krishna laughed, "You nailed it! It's the rare individual who is totally good or passionate or ignorant. There's a shade of grey in most individuals."

# The Topsy-Turvy Banyan Tree

Krishna continued, "There's this mythical topsy-turvy banyan tree which has its roots upward and its branches down. Its leaves are the spiritual knowledge. Very few souls are able to figure out what this tree is about. The branches of this tree are spread everywhere and it gets it nourishment from the three modes of material nature. The twigs are the sense objects and there are some roots going down as they are attached to the fruitive action of living beings."

Arjuna inquired, "Can we see this tree?"

Krishna answered, "This tree cannot be perceived by anyone. No one knows its beginning or end or where its foundation is. Only the weapon of detachment can cut this tree. Does this make sense?"

Arjuna replied, "O, Krishna, I get it! You're talking in allegorical language. The tree is us shackled to the three modes of nature. A person shackled to the three modes of nature is in an inverted position symbolized by the topsy-turvy banyan tree.

If you need to stand upright then you need to be detached to free yourself from the three modes of nature."

Krishna agreed, "Arjuna, you surprise me. I'm truly impressed that you figured out about the topsy-turvy tree. A truly detached person, who is not affected by happiness or sorrow and free from ego, lusty desires, self-grandeur and false association, will ever be lop-sided.

The Universal Consciousness, where all souls came from, should be the ultimate destination for realized souls. It's a place which is not illuminated by the sun, moon, stars or any other light source. It's a supremely blissful peace.

All souls who voted to play in the Game of Life and are finding the going tough should learn the art of detachment in order to be free and return back to me."

A soul is forced by its mind to play the Game of Life.

The mind chooses a family in which the soul takes birth. When the physical body dies, the soul quits the body to be reborn in another. In each body, he gets to enjoy different situations. Most people don't believe this. They do not think of themselves as an immortal soul residing in the physical body and they continue to play the Game of Life until they can take it no more and self-realization dawns on them."

Arjuna inquired, "What about you, Lord?"

Krishna laughs, "Hmm! The Supreme Soul is the source of everything in the material universe. He is omnipotent, omnipresent and omniscient. The Supreme Soul is situated in every person beside his soul and acts as the **higher self** or **divine observer** or **conscience** or **inner voice**. The Supreme Soul though residing in the physical body is beyond the three modes of nature and is not affected by them. Actions do not cling to the Supreme Soul because he is not attached to their results. Those who understand this and practice it live in freedom."

## Divine and Demonic Beings

Krishna continued, "In this world there are two types of beings- the **divine** and the **demonic**.

A divine person has most of the following qualities- fearlessness, purity of heart, charitable nature, clarity of mind and action, sense control, sacrificing, knowledge of the laws of the universe, austere, virtuous, non-violent, honest, cool-headed, compassionate, modest, hygienic, devoid of greed and jealousy and optimistic.

The demonic qualities are- pride, lust, arrogance, ego, anger, restlessness, unhygienic and ignorance. Individuals who are demonic cannot distinguish between right and wrong. They are atheists and severely criticize God and his creation. These people have high sexual desires and low self-control. They try to mess up everybody's life at the slightest pretext.

Some demonical individuals are so addicted to gaining material wealth that they do not hesitate to use unfair means to achieve their means.

They do not tolerate anybody coming in the way of their ambitions and will try to destroy their perceived enemies. These people have such huge egos; they feel they are the lords of everything. Then there are those who after amassing huge wealth by unfair means try to ease their nagging conscience (the Supreme Soul talking to them) by doing charity. They feel this "good deed" will help to erase their bad deeds."

Arjuna inquired, "What happens to such souls? Do they have any hope of salvation?"

Krishna spoke gravely, "Be on guard against such qualities. It's very difficult to get rid of demonical qualities once you acquire it. Such people do not feel the need to redeem themselves and attain salvation. They love the Game of Life and take repeated births in families that will encourage their evil qualities. Finally they will sink to the most abominable position of existence.

Finally, there are **three gates of hell- lust, anger and greed**.

Stay away from these qualities if you desire to exit the Game of Life."

## The Divisions of Faith

Arjuna said, "Who do individuals in the various modes of nature worship?"

Krishna replied, "Good question! Individuals in the mode of goodness worship the demigods. Those in the mode of passion worship the demons and those in mode of darkness worship the dead and ghosts."

Arjuna spoke, "Makes sense. What happens to individuals who do not follow the religious scriptures?"

Krishna answered, "There are some souls who undergo severe penances and austerities not mentioned in the spiritual books. It's their pride, egoism, lust attachments arising out of the modes of passion that goads them to do this. Some are so sadomasochistic that they try to torture their souls and the Super Soul residing within. It gives them perverse pleasures. They are the world's greatest fools."

Arjuna inquired, "What role does **food** play in shaping the quality of our lives?"

Krishna answered, "Foods in the mode of goodness increase the duration of life, improve health, increase strength and make you happy and satisfied. Such foods are tasty, contain essential nutrition and beneficial for the mind and body.

Foods that are too hot; too pungent; too salty or too sour will cause mental and physical imbalance. These foods tend to increase sexual desires in some.

Stale, tasteless, juiceless, rotting foods which have a bad smell are preferred by people in the mode of ignorance."

Arjuna continued, "What's the connection between the modes of nature and **following religious** and **spiritual principles**?"

Krishna replied, "If an individual follows the scriptures as a matter of duty and with no desire for material results, he is said to be in the mode of goodness.

If a person performs rituals and uses religion and spiritual as a means of gaining fame or material wealth, he is said to be in the mode of passion.

If an individual has no faith in the scriptures and does not follow the masters and is an unbeliever, he is considered to be in the mode of ignorance."

Arjuna asked, "What does **austerity** mean?"

Krishna answered, "Austerity means-

- Worshipping the Supreme Lord, following the advice of genuine spiritual gurus, parents and responsible adults.
- Cleanliness, leading a simple life, celibacy and believing in non-violence.
- Having control over one's speech by not saying hurtful and blasphemous things.
- Reading the holy books.
- Leading a satisfied, simple, pure and controlled life.

Arjuna persisted, "**Penance**?

Krishna spoke, "If an individual performs penance without expectation of material benefits but only for the sake of the Supreme Soul or the Universal Consciousness, it is said to be penance in the mode of goodness.

Penance performed to gain respect, honor or fame is called penance in the mode of passion. This penance has no lasting benefits.

Penance performed without direction, through self-tortures or by troubling others is said to be penance in the mode of ignorance or darkness."

Arjuna questioned, "What about **charity**?

Krishna replied, "Charity given to a worthy person or cause or organization in the proper place, time, circumstance and without expecting any benefits from the giving is said to be charity in the mode of goodness.

Charity performed grudgingly, with expectations of fame and benefits is said to be charity in the mode of passion.

Charity given to undesirable people, unworthy cause or organization without giving a thought to the end result is said to be charity in the mode of ignorance."

Krishna continued, "There's the mantra "**OM TAT SAT**" used to indicate the Supreme Absolute Truth. Let me tell you the significance of this mantra.

Before commencing any religious work, charity or penance intone "OM." This will connect you with the Universal Consciousness.

Then say "TAT." This will help you to be free from material attachments.

Finally the word "SAT." This indicates the objective of your divine activity.

Thus, performing religious activities, charities and penance with faith in the Supreme Soul will help the individual travel on the pathway of self-realization."

# Renunciation, Knowledge, Work, Workers, Happiness

Arjuna questioned, "O Supreme Lord! What's the purpose of renunciation and leading a renounced life?"

Krishna spoke, "Renunciation means not hankering after results. This state of "Desirelessness" is called the renounced order of life by the mystics."

Arjuna interrupted, "There are some gurus who are against renunciation."

Krishna laughed, "You get all types of advice. Some teach that giving up all fruitive activities is the way to go while others feel sacrifice, charity and penance will benefit you.

Dear Arjuna, don't forego religion, charity or penance. They must be followed by all intelligent persons and are very beneficial. Perform these activities as a matter of duty without expectation of any benefits.

Do not shirk from the duties which you have to carry out in your daily life. Perform your prescribed duties without pondering over the results. This renunciation is said be in the mode of goodness.

There are **five causes** in the accomplishment of any kind of work- **the place of action; the doer; the senses; the activity** and finally **the Super Soul**.

Whether an individual acts with his mind, body or speech, his actions, whether right or wrong, are constituted of the aforementioned five elements. If an individual thinks that he is the only doer while ignoring the five elements, he is considered to be a very confused person.

There are **three stimuli** to action- **knowledge, the object of knowledge** and **the knower**. There are **three factors** in the accomplishment of work- **the senses, the work** and **the doer**. Let me now explain the different kinds of knowledge, work and the workers.

If an individual sees every other soul as a part of the Universal Consciousness, his knowledge is understood to be in the mode of goodness.

If an individual thinks there are different kinds of souls in different types of living beings then his knowledge is in the mode of passion.

If an individual has very limited knowledge of his Self, the Game of Life and about the Universal Consciousness, then his knowledge is said to be in the mode of ignorance."

Arjuna spoke, "I get it. You've told me this before. All souls have come from a common source- the Universal Consciousness. We are all a part of you, Lord!"

Krishna smiled, "Thank you, Arjuna! Let's talk about **work**.

Work which is as per rules and regulations and performed without attachment, love or hatred and without any desire for results is called work in the mode of goodness.

Work carried out by individuals to satisfy one's ego and ambitions with a desire to achieve results is said to be work in the mode of passion.

Work which disregards the rules and regulations, which causes harm to nature and society and carried out with reckless abandon is said to be work in the mode of ignorance."

Arjuna inquired, "How does one attain perfection in his work?"

Krishna answered, "If an individual worships the Supreme Soul with devotion, he becomes perfect while doing his work. Never be envious about other people's occupation and the rewards he is getting for his job. It might not be right for you. Be satisfied with the work you do and remain unattached to the results from your efforts. You'll be a happy person.

Now, let's discuss the **workers**.

A worker who performs his work, without any ego or expectations of results from his activities is said to be a worker in the mode of goodness.

A worker who is obsessed with work and ensuing results and wants to enjoy the fruits of his labor is said to be a worker in the mode of passion. Such individuals are usually envious, extremely competitive and affected by joys and sorrows.

A worker who is materialistic, an idle dreamer, a con artist or indulges in unlawful activities is said to be a worker in the mode of ignorance."

Arjuna agreed.

Krishna continued, "Let's discuss **people** and **determination** according to the three modes.

If an individual is able to figure out which action is right and which is wrong, what is safe and what is unsafe and what causes bondage and what is liberating, he is said to be in the mode of goodness.

An individual who has incomplete understanding of the rules and regulations; can't distinguish between religion and irreligion and is confused by what should be done and what not to be done is said to be in the mode of passion.

An individual who considers irreligion to be religion and vice versa; who is deluded and always on the wrong side of the law is said to be in the mode of ignorance.

An individual with firm determination and self-control is said to be determined in the mode of goodness.

An individual who uses determination for material benefits is said to be in the mode of passion.

An individual who is an idle dreamer, always fearful, negative, pessimistic is said to be determined in the mode of ignorance. This person will never show any determination anywhere and anytime."

Arjuna inquired, "Lord, can **happiness** be classified under the three modes?"

Krishna answered, "Yes! It's possible to categorize happiness under the three modes.

Pleasure from the senses seems like nectar at first, but it is bitter as poison in the end.

That which seems like poison at first, but tastes like nectar in the end – this is the joy of existence, born of a mind at peace with itself. An individual experiencing happiness resulting in self-realization is said to be experiencing happiness in the mode of goodness.

An individual, who initially experiences through sense gratification but regrets later, is said to be experiencing happiness in the mode of passion.

An individual who experiences happiness by day-dreaming, sleeping or lazing about is said to be experiencing happiness in the mode of ignorance."

# Lessons from the Bhagavad Gita

Krishna spoke, "I'm done, Arjuna! Lecture session is over. I have shared profound truths with you, dear friend. Those who are able to figure out what I said will attain wisdom; they will follow the right principles to attain salvation. I gave you these precious words of wisdom; reflect on them and then do as you choose."

Arjuna said, "Lord, the divine knowledge you imparted was overwhelming. I beseech you. Please, could you put in a nutshell what you told me so far? I need a rehash to get the facts straight."

Krishna lectured, "I will summarize the key points of our discussion, for your benefit. Listen intently-

- The Super Soul or the Supreme Soul or the Universal Consciousness is omnipotent, omnipresent and omniscient. He is a field of energy and intelligence. He is the creator, sustainer as well the destroyer of the universe.

- Though the Supreme Soul is an impartial observer of the Game of Life, he is sometimes compelled to manifest a form (avatar) to release innocent people from tyrannical conditions on earth.
- You're an immortal soul residing in a physical body and playing a role in the Game of Life.
- The soul experiences the various stages of the body like birth, childhood, adulthood, old age and death. Once it completes a life cycle, it leaves its present body and goes on to reside in a new body. This goes on and on throughout eternity. This cycle is called "Reincarnation" or the "Game of Life."
- The ultimate destination of the soul is to merge with the Universal Consciousness, a place from where it originally came, and live in eternal bliss.
- A soul is neither created nor destroyed.
- A soul playing the Game of Life is affected by the three modes of nature- goodness > passion

> ignorance. Every soul and its actions can be described by any of these three modes.
- Only the Supreme Soul or the Universal Consciousness and self-realized souls are not affected by the three modes of nature.
- You should not fear death. Death is just a transitory phase.
- Souls, after death, who have played the game well- in the mode of goodness, get to enjoy heavenly pleasures in the heavenly planets for a long time until they return back to Earth to play the Game of Life.
- Souls, who have played the game in the mode of passion, take birth in families sharing similar tendencies.
- Souls, who have lead evil lives, go to the hellish planets, after death, where they become slaves of the demonic inhabitants. After suffering there for a long time they take births in primitive tribes or messed up families.
- Then, there are the souls who have become self-realized. They have carried out their

prescribed duties, without attachment to results of their actions. They get to live with me, in eternal salvation, after they leave their physical bodies.

- Do not run away from your prescribed duties. It is just not possible to be inactive while living in this material world. So, do your work without any expectations and you'll be a very happy individual.
- Trying to renounce various physical actions by leading the life of a monk, whilst your mind is forever thinking "dirty," is not going to help you at all to achieve self-realization.
- The Super Soul is seated beside the individual soul in every living physical body. The Super Soul acts as the conscience or inner voice. Learn to connect with the Higher Self, listen to your inner voice and follow his advice. You'll be happy.
- Stay away from lust, anger and greed. These qualities are the gateway to hell.

- Eat the right foods, practice charity, penance and sacrifice without any expectations. This will help you exit the Game of Life and merge with the Supreme.
- The key to self-realization is "Desirelesnness"

Does this make sense? What's your feedback?

Arjuna bowed before the Lord and said, "I can't thank you enough, Lord! What an awesome interactive session it was! I'm on the way to self-realization. I'm so blessed to have you as my eternal friend. I'm free from all self-doubts. I'm a warrior and am ready to fight. I'll do so with the realization that fighting is my prescribed duty. I shall do so without thinking about the outcome."

Krishna concluded, "I'm with you, Arjuna!"

Sanjaya spoke, "Sire! Lord Krishna' divine sermon has concluded. I'm awestruck by what I heard. It was so enlightening. I'm so happy. I've now become a true believer of the Supreme Soul and will follow the path of self-realization."

# Uddhava Gita

## Lord Krishna and Uddhava

The Uddhava Gita is a dialogue between **Lord Krishna**, the incarnation of the Supreme **Lord Vishnu**, and his devotee and friend, **Uddhava**. This spiritual discussion took place just before the Lord's departure to his heavenly kingdom, **Vaikuntha**.

It's been 30 years since Lord Krishna narrated the Bhagavad Gita to Arjuna on the battlefield of Kurukshetra. The war was over. The Kauravas and their kin were totally destroyed. The Pandavas won and the eldest Pandava, Yudhisthira, became the king of Hastinapura. After that, Lord Krishna returned to his kingdom Dwaraka. However, good times did not last long.

The destruction of Lord Krishna's clan, the **Yadavas**, was imminent. The Yadavas had been cursed by **Queen Gandhari** and the holy sages. The curse was that the Yadavas would start fighting amongst themselves and totally destroy each other. This was as per the Lord's wish. The Yadavas had gotten very arrogant and if they were unchecked they would have destroyed civilization.

Lord Krishna assembles the Yadava nobles and advises them to take their men to a place called **Prabhasa** and perform rituals for the benefit of the clan. This strategy would turn out to be the starting point for the Yadavas' annihilation.

Uddhava overheard the conversation and he was totally scared. He could not figure out why Lord Krishna had assembled the Yadavas and asked them to go to Prabhasa. He wondered why he was not asked to accompany the Yadava men. He feared for his safety, after his master's departure. He spills out his fears before the Lord.

The Lord assuages his fears. Uddhava then requests for spiritual guidance. The Lord responds by discussing the Game of Life, self-realization, the awesome yoga technique for merging with the Supreme, the mystic powers, the mysteries of creation and the vagaries of the mind. Uddhava becomes spiritually enlightened and brave after listening to the Lord's words.

Let's start-

**Lord Brahma**- the God of Creation, **Lord Shiva**- the God of Destruction and celestial beings from other planets descended on Earth to meet with Lord Krishna. They stood before the Lord, in his palace, with heads bowed and greeted him with a **Namaste**.

Lord Brahma, on behalf of the assembled group, addressed the Lord, "One hundred and twenty five years ago, O Supreme Lord Vishnu, you took birth in the Yadava clan as Lord Krishna, to purge the world of evil. You have achieved what you had come for. We have seen your mighty deeds to establish righteousness here.

You taught your followers how to play the **Game of Life** and achieve salvation. I guess there's nothing left for you to accomplish on earth.

Your earthly race, the Yadavas, have grown arrogant and aggressive due to the wealth and support they received under your rule and are now doomed to total annihilation. This is the effect of the curse they received from the holy men they tormented. We know you will let the curse run its course.

Please, O Divine Lord, it's time you returned back to your transcendent kingdom, Vaikuntha, which is beyond all the material universes and take care of us."

Krishna spoke, "Thank you, dear Brahma, for your kind words. I am glad to inform you that I have already taken the decision of leaving this planet.

The Yadavas have become drunk with power and are trying to conquer the world. As long as I am here, they are powerless to do much harm. Hence, I have decided upon a strategy to bring about their annihilation before returning to my kingdom."

Brahma said, "We are pleased to hear that you will be returning to Vaikuntha soon. Please accept our prayers and allow us to return to our worlds."

Brahma and his group members then departed to their world. Lord Krishna called all the Yadava nobles and addressed them, "You are well aware of the curse uttered by the holy men and the effect it is having on our clan members. You need to hurry up and send all your women, children and the old people to the holy place called **Shankoddara**.

Thereafter, you and your men go to Prabhasa, which is a sacred place on the river **Ganges**. Perform rituals and acts of charity to counteract the ill effects of the curse."

The Yadavas, heeding Lord Krishna's advice, went to Prabhasa and performed a fire sacrifice. During the rituals, the Yadava men drank an intoxicating beverage that made them forget everything, their identities, their relatives etc. Being intoxicated, by the will of the Lord, they fought with each other, and the result was the annihilation of the Yadavas.

## Uddhava Pleads with Lord Krishna

Uddhava bowed before the Lord and pleaded, "O, Master! I heard what Lord Brahma was discussing with you. I guess you are about to leave this world. Your absence will seal the fate of our Yadava clan. They will be doomed to extinction.

What about me?

Lord, I have been your devotee, friend and attendant and if you leave me here, I am a goner.

What's life without you?

I beseech you to please take me with you."

Krishna spoke, "Dear Uddhava, it's true what you said. I am done with my worldly duties and so, I am returning to my heavenly realm.

I restored righteousness in this world and I am done here.

Yes! The Yadava clan is going to be destroyed and my kingdom, Dwaraka, will disappear under the sea within the next seven days."

My kingdom was created by me and so will cease to exist after I am gone.

Evil will rise again and the **Dark Age of Kali** will begin. Evil will reign supreme and goodness will be subjugated in the future."

Uddhava croaks, "OMG! I am totally freaked out. What am I going to do?"

## The Illusory Universe

Krishna spoke, "Don't worry. You are my dearest devotee. I will protect you. I have sent the Yadava men to Prabhasa where they will battle with each other and get annihilated. You are safe from the holy men's curse.

I have a divine plan for you. However, you need to be spiritually evolved. Start by practicing detachment. Think of all this happenings as an illusion. Fix your mind on me. Do not allow your mind to wander elsewhere. Stay focused.

Remember your true identity as the immortal soul residing in this illusory physical body. See this entire universe as an image created by the **Universal Consciousness**. Everything's a mirage. You will feel peaceful. The Universal Consciousness pervades everywhere and this omnipresent, omnipotent and omniscient presence is me.

If you believe what I say, you will realize that everything's an illusion and the only reality is the soul residing inside all living beings.

This divine knowledge will free you from the Game of Life or the cycle of births and deaths."

Uddhava spoke, "Lord, what you said makes total sense but the truth is- I am an ordinary guy. All these years, I was totally attached to my physical body thinking it was real. I was possessive of my family and hankered after worldly possessions. The concept of "I" and "mine" is deeply embedded in me and I am stuck with it.

You are now asking me to be detached. It's very difficult to let go of all that I cherished in my life.

So, Master, tell me how I can carry out your instructions."

Krishna answered, "I know where that's coming from. It's difficult to make a life-change but you need to do it. You are the not first person who will be trying this.

There are many individuals in this world who have realized their true identity and ceased longing for material benefits. They have figured out that this material world is nothing but an illusion created by the Universal Consciousness.

On this planet, it is the souls of human beings which have the ability to realize this supreme truth. Other living beings are not so lucky.

So, why not give self-realization a try?"

## The King and the Young Man

Krishna saw the skeptic look on Uddhava's face and spoke, "Let me make this easy for you. I will now tell you the parable of a **king and the self-realized young man**.

One day, a king was passing through the woods when he saw a young, radiant man wandering about aimlessly. The king was a wise man and he figured out that this person was no ordinary soul. He decided to test whether his assumptions were true or not.

He addressed the young man, "Hey, lad! Apparently, you look like an intelligent person but your carefree behavior suggests otherwise. Most people have goals in life and work hard to achieve them. You seem totally oblivious to your surroundings and at the same time you have the look of a blissful person. What's your secret?"

The young man smiled and replied, "O King! I can sense your confusion. I am what I am because of the many awesome teachers I had. I learned a lot from them. They are the secret of my happiness."

The king was curious. He inquired, "Who are these awesome teachers?"

The young man answered, "I had 25 teachers who taught me everything. Don't laugh out loud when I tell you who they are. They are: **earth; air; space; water; fire; sun; moon; dove; python; ocean; moth; bee; elephant; honey gatherer; deer; fish; whore; osprey; infant; maiden; arrow smith; serpent; tree; wasp and my body.**"

The king was confused, "Does not make any sense. Please explain."

# The 25 Teachers

The young man replied, "O King! Listen carefully-

**1. Earth:** The earth taught me to be undisturbed by anything. Whatever be the terrestrial or extraterrestrial disturbances, the earth continues with its rotations around itself and revolutions around the sun. It never deviates from its path nor slows down, come what may. I decided that I, too, will be like the earth. I will never be perturbed by any disturbances around me. My goal will be to serve others and I shall never deviate from this goal.

**2. Air:** The constituents of air are perfectly balanced to sustain life on earth. If there are serious imbalances then all living things will soon become extinct. Air moves freely about and is in contact with everything on this planet. It is not attached to anything. It goes inside our lungs and comes out without expecting any reward or punishment from us. The gentle breeze carries fragrance or stench from place to place. It does not show any discrimination between good smells and bad smells.

The air has taught me to be balanced in life. It has taught me not to be affected by the happenings in this material world. So, all things, good or bad, have ceased to affect me.

The Universal Consciousness is like the air. It pervades everywhere and is a part of me, the Self. This realization has made me blissful.

**3. Space:** Just as the space remains untouched by the form it fills, I figured out the Self should also remain untouched by the physical body it occupies.

**4. Water:** Water is transparent, pure and sweet. It cleanses and purifies anything washed with it. Life cannot survive without water.

I learned that I should be transparent in my feelings and dealings with other living beings. My goal should be self-realization and helping others to realize their true identities.

It's the gateway to eternal salvation.

**5. Fire:** Fire burns brightly or it can be hidden like the fire in our bellies, which digests the food we eat. Fire has the power to take the form of any object which it has engulfed.

It has the power to extract pure metal from the ore in which it hides.

The Self is like the fire which burns brightly. The Self has the power to burn up all impure thoughts and deeds and become pure. The Self, like fire, takes the shape of the physical body it occupies.

**6. Sun:** The Sun taught me non-attachment to material objects. Just as the sun is responsible for life on this planet but is not attached to terrestrial objects, the Self which resides in a physical body should not get attached to it.

The sun's ray's evaporates sea water which forms clouds and these clouds condense as rain, soon after. A yogi should emulate the sun. If he is enlivened by happy incidents, he should not bask in it. He should realize everything in this material world is temporary and be grounded.

The reflection of the sun in water is not the sun. Likewise this universe is but a reflection in the Universal Consciousness.

**7: Moon:** The moon appears to change its shape due to the shadow of the earth falling on it but in reality it is forever ovoid in shape. The earth's shadow has no effect on the true shape of the moon.

Likewise, the Self should observe the Game of Life (cycle of births and deaths) dispassionately and not change its outlook. The moon taught me to remain unchanged in spite of the changing circumstances in my life.

The Self should also be unaffected by the happenings in the material world.

**8. Dove:** The dove taught me a valuable lesson. If you are going to be attached to material objects then there's always some pain associated with it.

Let me illustrate by telling you a story of the Dove family.

Not far from here, there lived Mr. Dove on a tree. Mr. Dove got married and he was very besotted with Mrs. Dove. Mrs. Dove also loved Mr. Dove very much. They were a happy couple. He made love to her often and tried to fulfill all her wishes, however difficult they might be.

He assembled a cozy nest for them.

Very soon, Mrs. Dove laid three eggs. Mr. Dove was ecstatic. He was going to be a father of three chicks. The eggs soon hatched and three hungry chicks came crying out. Mrs. Dove fed them and took good care of them. Mr. Dove searched the forest for food and flew home often to check out whether everything was okay in his household.

One day, Mr. Dove asked Mrs. Dove to accompany him. It was a long time since he had made love to her. His spouse was too busy looking after the chicks that she hardly noticed him. Mrs. Dove did not feel like leaving the chicks alone in the nest but she also loved her spouse very much to refuse him. Off, they flew away to enjoy physical pleasures.

It so happened, a fowler was on the prowl looking for birds to trap and eat. His gaze fell upon the dove's nest and the three chicks in it. He cast his nest over the nest and trapped the chicks in it.

Call it motherly instinct, Mrs. Dove felt very uneasy and she requested her spouse that she would like to return to the nest.

He agreed and she flew back to their nest. Shocker! The nest was in shambles and her chicks were trapped in the fowler's nest. She tried to rescue her chicks and got entangled in the meshes of the net.

Mr. Dove returned soon after and he saw his beloved spouse and chicks trapped in the fowler's nest. He cooed loudly. "Why the heck did I ask Mrs. Dove to accompany me? Why was I so lustful? Look, what's happened now? I was so busy with my self-interests that I threw caution to the winds." So saying, Mr. Dove got himself deliberately entangled in the net.

The fowler returned and took the Dove family to his house. His family had a hearty meal of dove meat.

This incident taught me never to be lustful or be besotted by the opposite sex. There's only trouble ahead. There's only one final result in this material world. It's death. So, why hanker after temporary objects of pleasure?

**9. Python:** Have you observed a python? It does not chase its prey. It waits patiently for the prey to come very near to it.

Then, it springs into action and coils itself around its hapless prey and asphyxiates it. The python is also capable of remaining without food for days.

A wise person should not hanker for things beyond his grade. He should wait for and accept whatever his fate throws at him and be satisfied with it. There could be days when nothing seems to go right. He should accept the downturn in his fortunes and patiently wait for the good times to come over.

**10. Ocean:** The Ocean is calm and tranquil. When there's a storm brewing over it, the waters churn and the ocean appears agitated. The storm subsides and the ocean is calm again.

I try to be like the ocean. Sometimes, some incidents freak me out. Then, I immediately remind myself that I am the Self and should not be perturbed by happenings in this material world. This reality helps me to be calm and tranquil like the ocean.

**11. Moth:** I don't know, what's with moths? They are forever attracted to a bright flame and get burned.

Most people are like moths.

They don't seem to let go of material pleasures even when they know it's temporary and can cause misery.

I always remember the moth whenever I am tempted and thus remain safe.

**12. Bee:** Bees gather nectar from different flowers to make sweet honey. A wise person should also read different scriptures and take the essence of the teachings from these books.

Bees make honey and hoard it. What happens? A honey gatherer comes and steals the honey from them. A wise man should not keep his knowledge to himself. He should impart this knowledge to others before death arrives and his knowledge is lost.

O King! Knowledge is to be shared. I share my knowledge with whoever cares to listen and this makes me very happy.

**13. Elephant:** A mighty elephant does not try to break the tiny rope, which its trainer has tied to its foot, and run away. Likewise, most people find it difficult to run away from lust and vices.

It's so easy to unshackle yourself from the world of miseries. If a person remembers his true Self and the illusory nature of the material world, he will be truly free.

**14. Honey Gatherer:** A honey gatherer goes to the forest with the sole intention of gathering honey. He is focused in his goal. At the same time, he is also on the lookout for dangers that might cause him grave harm.

Our ultimate goal in this Game of Life should be self-realization and attainment of supreme bliss. At the same time, we must be wary of temptations that can lure us away from our goal.

**15. Deer:** The shy deer can be lured into a trap if you act friendly and offer it grass. At first, it will hesitate. If you keep at it, it becomes comfortable with your presence and starts approaching you. Finally, it will eat the grass offered by you. You can then tether the deer.

If you need to come out of this never ending cycle of births and deaths, you need to stay away from temptations that lure you with fake promises.

Ignore them.

If you are drawn towards the objects of temptation then there's no turning back. You are trapped! You will be experiencing only temporary happiness. After reality sinks in, it's going to be too late. You will be tethered to worldly temptations and miseries.

**16. Fish:** What happened to the fish that got greedy and bit on the fisherman's hook? It became the fisherman's food! We must learn not to be greedy and "bite more than we can chew." This can prove to be our undoing.

The sense of taste is the most empowering among all the senses. Eating lots of food can cause health problems. Eat a quantity which is enough to sustain you in your daily activities. Do not start the habit of eating rich food. It's not good for one's health. What will happen to you if it's not available or you can't afford it?

I eat whatever I get and am not sniffy about the quality of food. Learn to control your sense of taste and you are on the path of self-realization.

**17. Whore:** There was a whore. Her name was Pingala. She was beautiful and knew how to please her customers. Pingala had a dream- One day, a rich customer will come to sleep with her and she will satisfy his wildest fantasies. He will be so happy that he will take her home and make her his wife.

Alas! That fantasy remained a day-dream. Pingala waited for many years for a rich man to take her away. The sad truth- Hundreds of customers came, paid her, satisfied their lust and went away. Nobody bothered to look upon her as a person.

Pingala soon realized this sad fact and she wailed, "Why did I pursue this impossible dream? What a fool I was, to expect redemption from clients who only wanted to satisfy their lust? I forgot I was the immortal soul and my love should have been God or the Universal Consciousness. If I had loved him and prayed to him to deliver me from this world of miseries, he would never have let me down."

From that day, Pingala stopped being a whore. She became a self-realized soul and attained salvation.

Whenever I get lofty dreams, I remember Pingala and wake up. I am totally grounded.

**18. Osprey:** An osprey was carrying flesh in its beak. A larger osprey saw this and started to snatch the flesh from the smaller bird. End result- The bigger bird won!

In this material world, most people try to win at other people's cost. There's lots of unhappiness trying to be a success in this illusory world.

What's the point of playing worldly games, when you know it's not real? Why compete in a game where the bigger and better person wins at the expense of his less fortunate brethren?

I decided not to participate in the Game of Life. I rejoice in the beauty of my Self and am forever happy.

**19. Infant:** An infant has no worries. It instinctively knows its parents will take care of it.

I am like the infant. I am free from all worries because I know the Supreme Lord will take care of me.

**20. Maiden:** There was a young, beautiful girl.

Her parents had gone out and she was all alone in the house. During this time, some of her relatives arrived to discuss some family matters with her parents. She invited them in and informed them that her parents would be back soon.

She then went to the kitchen, to prepare some snacks for the guests. Crikey! She had worn many gold bangles on each hand and they were jingling when she was preparing the dishes. What would the guests say? The girl removed all the bangles save one each on either wrist. She could now work silently.

I learned a lesson from this parable- If many people live together, there's going to be lots of talk and squabbles. Forget a larger group, even couples fight. I decided never to live with any person. It's good to be single. No useless talks and fights.

I lead a peaceful, solitary life. I practice meditation every day.

I meditate as follows-

I sit in a comfortable position. I take deep breaths.

I then silence my mind by counting my intakes and outtakes of air from my lungs. I do this till my mind stops its useless chatter. After that, I revel in the beauty of the Self.

It's an awesome experience!

**21. Arrowsmith:** The arrowsmith was so focused on preparing the perfect arrows for his prized client that he hardly noticed the king passing by with loud fanfare.

If you need to be self-realized and be free from the cycle of births and deaths, then stay focused and don't get distracted by the temptations around you.

**22. Serpent:** A snake inhabits a hole that others have dug and left.

I have never constructed a house for myself. I stay in a place which provides me safety and shelter, be it a cave, tree or an abandoned dwelling. Thus, I have no worries of looking after the house and spending money on it.

**23. Tree:** A tree provides shelter and food to everybody even if a person or animal tries to damage it. It remains firmly grounded.

I learned from the tree to be loving and caring to all beings even if some of them hurt you. I am fully grounded with the knowledge that nobody can harm me since I am the immortal soul or the Self. The Self is immortal and nothing can ever harm it.

**24. Wasp:** The wasp begins its life cycle as an egg. From the egg, emerges the larva. The larva does not resemble the wasp. The larva has primordial knowledge that it will soon turn into a wasp. It happens. The wasp then leaves its nest and flies away.

I am not the physical body (larva). I am the immortal Self. I should be free from the cycle of births and deaths and fly away to be one with the Supreme Soul or the Universal Consciousness.

**25. My Body:** My body also taught me many things. Since it has taken birth, it's also going to die one day. The body is the source of unhappiness. It is also a great teacher. I reside within it and it has shown me that nothing in this material world is permanent. So, why waste time playing the game of births and deaths which give no lasting happiness?

What happens to the body when the soul leaves it? It rots! So, why should I be body conscious?

I am the Self, indestructible and immortal. I must stop taking part in this stupid Game of Life and attain salvation.

These teachers helped me to be free from all worldly attachments. I am now carefree and fully established in the beauty of the Self. It would be impossible to learn all this from a single teacher. I hope, dear king, what I said made sense to you."

The king was enlightened by the young man's discourse and he bowed before him and said, "Thank you, wise guru. You have opened my eyes. I will practice what you have preached and try to attain self-realization."

Krishna concluded the story, "The king returned to his palace a totally changed person."

## Game of Life

Uddhava spoke, "Dear Lord! That was an awesome, thought-provoking tale. Now, please explain how ignorant souls continue to accept roles in the Game of Life."

Krishna answered, "The mind, which is easily enamored by worldly pleasures and things, contemplates the objects of the senses that are found in this world and the other worlds. Taking the helpless soul (Self) with it, the mind travels everywhere in search of new worldly experiences. Thus, the soul is trapped by the mind into playing the Game of Life or the cycle of births and deaths.

When the soul quits its body to accept another body, as per the mind's diktat and the results of its past life actions (**karma**), it becomes accustomed to its new body and forgets everything that happened in its previous life. Death erases the experiences of one's previous life. Since the mind, which is in control of the senses, has chosen a new body, the soul accepts the new role and starts enacting it.

In this way, the Self becomes a confused participant in the Game of Life and foolishly identifies itself with the physical body.

The nine stages of life - conception, gestation, birth, infancy, childhood, youth, middle age, old age, and death only relate to the physical body and not the Self.

If one observes the cycles of birth and death around him and realizes that the physical body is not permanent but undergoes many changes and tribulations, he will no longer be interested in playing roles in the Game of Life A truly ignorant person, who considers the physical universe and everything in it to be real, continues to play the Game of Life.

If the soul plays its role in the mode of goodness then it takes future roles as sages or demigods until it becomes self-realized and quits the Game of Life to be with me forever.

If the soul plays its role in the mode of passion then depending upon the intensity of its actions it takes birth as human beings or demons.

If the soul plays its role in the mode of ignorance then depending upon the intensity of its actions it takes birth as lower class of beings or becomes a ghost.

Just as a fan, although not an actor, takes on the mannerisms of his favorite actor, the soul, although not actually the doer but merely a witness, becomes captivated by the temptations of the physical world and starts playing roles.

**Therefore, O Uddhava, wake up. Know who you are. Stop playing meaningless roles in the Game of Life and come back to me."**

## The Lord Instructs Brahma

Uddhava inquired, "Why do human beings act like idiots and persist in playing the Game of Life, in spite of knowing the ultimate result- misery and death?"

Krishna replied, "An ignorant person falsely identifies himself with his physical body and mind. Such a person is overwhelmed by the modes of passion and ignorance, making him susceptible to material longings and temptations. He is so caught up in the rat-race that he forgets such targets will eventually bring only unhappiness.

Such a person should ask his inner mind- Is it worth it? After figuring out the answer, he should change his outlook and learn to control his mind. He should practice yoga and realize there's no lasting happiness in playing the Game of Life. The true goal of the Self is to stop playing roles in the material world and be one with the Universal Consciousness where there is eternal bliss."

Uddhava asked, "Lord, please tell me about the science of self-realization which you taught the ancients."

Krishna spoke, "Long, long ago, Lord Brahma and the sages asked me whether there was a method by which a person, who desires liberation from the activities of sense gratification, could cutoff the link between the sense objects and the mind.

I appeared before them in the form of a swan. They were bewildered by my birdlike appearance. After they figured out my disguise, they settled down.

I replied, "If a person is serious about controlling his mind, then he should perceive all matter as a temporary illusion appearing within the mind. It's like a streaking circle of red created when you whirl a blazing stick.

When a soul comes to play the Game of Life, the modes of nature divide the soul's consciousness into three stages of perception- wakefulness, dreaming, and deep sleep. These perceptions are not real but illusions.

If a soul realizes the temporary and illusory nature of the material world, it should remain free from all material desires.

It should carry out its worldly activities without expectations of the outcome. Just as a drunk does not know whether he is clothed or naked, a self-realized soul does not notice whether its temporary body is sitting, standing, or walking about.

A self-realized soul, who has figured out the absolute reality, will never be a prisoner of the physical body and its manifestations, knowing it to be just like a body seen in a dream."

Krishna continued, "Lord Brahma and the sages were totally satisfied with this knowledge and thanked me for it. I then left for my heavenly abode."

## Task of a Devotee

Uddhava spoke, "Master! Thank you. I, too, am enlightened by your divine wisdom. Now, please tell me about the duties of a devotee."

Krishna smiled, "Hmm. Here goes-

- A true devotee indulges in devotional service;
- He takes refuge in me;
- He performs his daily duties without any expectation of results;
- He remembers his true identity- an immortal soul, the Self, residing in a physical body and playing a role in the Game of Life;
- A true devotee is free from envy, anger, jealousy and attachments to material pleasures;
- He does not indulge in idle talk;
- He sees the Lord situated in the hearts of all living beings;
- He has no body consciousness;
- He is righteous in his behavior;
- He follows the religious principles and obeys gurus who will guide him to his final destination- to be with me forever;

- A true devotee likes to talk about the Supreme Lord and his divine message."

Uddhava replied, "Awesome, Lord! What you disclosed will be a guidepost on the path of self-realization. Please tell me about genuine gurus and their followers."

Krishna answered, "A true guru is like a kindling at the base of the fire. The followers are like the wood placed on top. Teaching is what connects them. Together they produce a spark that lights up the fire of knowledge which brings joy to the listeners.

A true guru shows the path of self-realization.

A guru starts as a follower of another self-realized guru. After learning and practicing what was taught to him, he is anointed as a guru by his teacher. Thus, a follower becomes a guru."

Uddhava questioned, "What advice would you give to individuals who are in mindless pursuit of material success?"

Krishna answered, "There are individuals who will stop at nothing to achieve great material success.

They are ready to mow down anything which stands in their path of success.

What's the final result of all super achievers? Death! Have you seen any super successful person live forever? So, why hanker after something that is not lasting.

Instead, isn't it good if you do your assigned worldly duties without competing with others or hankering after results? You will be a lot happier if you practice "**desirelessness**."

**I am going to repeat this often**- True happiness is not found in this illusory universe. If an individual realizes that he is an immortal soul, whose final destination should be living with me in eternal bliss, rather than continuing to play the misery filled Game of Life here, he will be happy forever!"

## Being Detached

Uddhava inquired, "Lord, How can the soul live in a physical body and yet be detached?"

Krishna replied, "Let me illustrate your question with an example- An individual is like two birds sharing the same nest on a tree. One eats the fruits of the tree. The other does not. However, the one who does not eat the fruit is the source of strength for both.

That which is free (the soul) and that which is bound (the mind) have different qualities even though they share the same body. The soul is part of Reality. The mind has become a prisoner of the Game of Life and continues to play roles (eating the fruits of the tree) in the illusory world.

If the soul is able to shake off its attachment to the mind-body combination and remain a dispassionate witness to all the events within it and around it then it will regain its lost freedom.

Freeing oneself from the mental imaginations of happiness, sadness, ego, competitiveness, lust and other feelings without judging them as good or bad, right or wrong will unshackle the soul from its self-imposed prison.

In reality there's neither true bondage nor liberation. They're the delusions of the mind. There's no need to perform yogic or other meditative exercises, recite prayers or mantras, listen to guru-talk to achieve bliss and serenity of the Self.

All you need to do is to withdraw your mind from the objects of the senses and remember that you do not require these unreal objects of distraction and misery.

If you wish to be truly happy then you should strive to be desire-less, unattached with worldly things and just contemplate upon your inner Self.

If you control the activities of the body, mind and speech, you will start experiencing supreme bliss.

You will not be bothered by what's happening around you.

If you have understood the true illusory nature of this world, you will be nonplussed about the miserable conditions around you.

You must always remember your true identity (soul) and recognize the souls, residing in other entities. If you stop dissociating with your bodies then the problems associated with the body will hardly bother you."

## The Tree of Life

Uddhava inquired, "Dear Lord, what is the way out for individuals who do not- follow religious principles / perform rituals / read the religious scriptures / visit places of pilgrimage / perform charitable deeds?"

Krishna answered, "It is not necessary for a living being to do any of the activities you mentioned to achieve self-realization. There's an easy and surefire way out.

The association of pure devotees can destroy one's attachment to material life! Their knowledge and qualities will rub off on you and you will be spiritually uplifted.

Pure devotees will enlighten you with the following truths-

- I am the **Supersoul** situated in all living beings.
- By surrendering to my divine will, any living being will assuredly be freed from fear in all circumstances."

Krishna continued, "The Supreme Lord is situated within the hearts of all living beings. It is only by his presence that the physical body is animated.

It should be understood that the mental, physical and spiritual functions of the body are all my materially manifest form.

**Have you been to a farm?**

What's the common link between all the plants that grow there?

The soil!

Likewise, the Supersoul or the Universal Consciousness is the common link between all souls.

**Do you know what the Tree of Life is?**

This Tree of Life is the manifestation of the Universal Consciousness. It is made up of-

- Pure and impurity are its two seeds;
- The unlimited material desires are its roots;
- The three modes of material nature; mode of goodness; mode of passion and mode of ignorance are its trunk;
- The five material elements are its branches;
- The eleven senses are its sub-branches;

- The five sense objects are its sap;
- Air, bile, and mucus are its three layers of bark;
- Happiness and misery are its fruits;
- The Supersoul and the individual soul are the two birds that live in this tree;
- This tree extends up to the sun;
- Ignorant beings enjoy one of the fruits of this tree (misery), and self-realized individuals enjoy the other fruit (happiness).

**Be self-realized and eat the fruit of happiness."**

## Different Gurus, Different Philosophies

Uddhava asked, "Lord, various gurus have prescribed variety of methods for achieving the ultimate goal of life. Are all these methods correct? Is there a superior technique?

Your recipe was devotional service, by which one can free himself from all material desires and attain salvation."

Krishna answered, "The illusory universe undergoes a cycle of creation and dissolution. So, whenever the universe is annihilated all knowledge is lost. Then, when the universe is recreated, I impart the knowledge to the gods, sages, and intelligent beings living in different worlds.

Each being absorbed the knowledge according to their capacity of assimilation and they presented their version to their successors. Thus, various philosophies have come into existence.

Some say that happiness is obtained as the result of performing pious activities.

Others say that gaining fame / wealth, enjoying worldly pleasures, being honest, controlling the senses, ritual work, giving in charity, austerity, or excelling at work are the causes of happiness. The followers of these methods achieve only temporary results for all their efforts. These methods cannot completely purify a person who is not devotional.

True happiness is achieved by one who has freed himself from all desires for material pleasures, and who is fully surrendered unto me. Thus, one who does not desire material pleasures, and who is peaceful, self-controlled, self-satisfied and does not discriminate between living beings finds only happiness wherever he goes. My devotees do not desire fame, wealth, mystic powers, or liberation from the Game of Life, because they have dedicated their lives to me. They are very dear to me."

Uddhava countered, "What if a devotee is not able to control his senses or commits some despicable deeds?"

Krishna replied, "O Uddhava, interesting question!

If my devotee is not able to control his senses he might be a little prone to material enjoyment, but since he is engaged in devotional service, he will not be diverted by these indulgences.

If my devotee commits a despicable deed due to situations beyond his control, he will still be my devotee because of his devotional service.

Let me illustrate with the following examples-

- A brave warrior is badly wounded in battle but he ignores the pain and goes on to win the battle.
- A person is afflicted by a terrible disease but he is cured with proper medical treatment.

Devotional service has the power to destroy the sinful reactions of my devotees, just as a fire has the power to burn firewood to ashes. With devotional service, my devotee is purified of all contamination caused by previous karmic activities and attains eternal bliss.

If a patient's eyes are infected, the eye-drops, prescribed by the physician, help cure his eyes problem and gain normal vision.

Likewise, a living being affected by the lure of material pleasures can be cured by hearing my divine discourses and praying.

One who is aware of his eternal self should stop thinking of women as sex objects because lust is a dangerous enemy of self-realization. Such interests only lead to mental and physical distress."

# The Ancient Yoga Meditational Technique

Uddhava spoke, "Lord, please describe to me how one should practice meditation. Does one need to use a form or image while meditating?"

Krishna lectured, "I will now describe to you a very powerful meditational technique which I taught the demigods, ancient sages and advanced beings that lived on this earth and other planets eons ago.

The meditation technique consists of two stages- **Stage I- Mindfulness of breathing** and **Stage II- Visualization of the God form and the Self.**

**Step I- Mindfulness of breathing**

**1.** Choose a place where there are no disturbances of any kind;

**2.** Sit on a level seat that is neither too high nor too low;

**3.** Keep the body straight so that the back, neck and head are in a straight line;

**4.** Check out whether you are comfortable in this position;

**5.** Placing the hands, palms upward, on your lap;

**6.** Focus the eyes on the tip of the nose;

**7.** Become aware of your breathing. Don't try to change it. Just feel it and observe it.

**8.** Inhale slowly and hold your breath in for a few seconds;

**9.** Focus your attention on the inhalation.

**10.** Now, exhale slowly and hold the breath out for a few seconds;

**11.** Focus your attention on the exhalation;

**12.** Do ten repetitions of this-inhale-focus-hold–exhale–focus-hold cycle during each session;

**13.** Practice this breathing technique, three times a day, for a month. The key is to focus on the intakes and outtakes of breath to still the mind. If your mind wanders, anytime during the activity, accept it as its nature and return to a consciousness of breathing;

**14.** Intoning the sacred word "OM" sonorously, while you exhale, might also help you steady your mind;

**15.** In one month, you should have enough control over your mind to start the visualization part of meditation.

**Step II- Visualization of the God Form and the Self**

**1.** Perform step I to silence the mind;

**2.** Stand facing north or east;

**3.** Keeping the eyes half or fully closed, gaze at the tip of the nose;

**4.** Visualize a white lotus bud situated within the heart. Do this exercise, for a few days, until you are able to see the image clearly in your mind's eye;

**5.** Now, see the lotus bud open up. It has eight petals and an erect stalk. Do this exercise, for a few days, until you are able to see the image clearly in your mind's eye;

**6.** Now, visualize the sun, moon, and fire; Do this exercise, for a few days, until you are able to see the image clearly in your mind's eye;

**7.** After you are able to see them clearly, place them one after another within the whorls of the lotus flower. Do this exercise, for a few days, until you are able to see the image clearly in your mind's eye;

**8.** Visualize my **divine form** (Check out the next two chapters for the descriptions of Lord Krishna and Lord Vishnu) or a God form, you believe in, at the center of the lotus and meditate on the form. Do this exercise, for a few days, until you are able to see the image clearly in your mind's eye;

**9.** Now focus your total attention on the divine face and hold on to it. Do this until you are only noticing the divine face in successive attempts;

**10.** Staying focused, let the form disappear and in its place, behold the Self (**a brilliant white dot**) of all. Let your whole being be absorbed by the Self and let it fill your entire being. Be absorbed in the Self like a fire uniting with fire;

**11.** If you reach this stage then you have become the **master of the illusory universe!**"

# Earthly Form of Lord Krishna

If your God form is Lord Krishna then this is how you will visualize him during your meditation-

**1.** Lord Krishna has a perfect body structure, and his face is beautiful and captivating;

**2.** He has two long arms, beautiful shoulders, a handsome forehead, a pure smile, and ears that are decorated with shark-shaped earrings;

**3.** He has a darkish complexion;

**4.** He is dressed in golden-yellowish garments;

**5.** Around the neck is a garland of flowers;

**6.** His head is adorned with an effulgent golden crown with a peacock feather stuck to it;

**7.** The feet are decorated with ankle bells;

**8.** The arms are decorated with gem studded bracelets;

**9.** A golden belt girdles the waist;

**10.** He carries a golden flute in his right hand.

## Transcendental Form of Lord Vishnu

If your God form is Lord Vishnu then this is how you will visualize him during your meditation-

**1.** Lord Vishnu has a perfect body structure, and his face is beautiful and captivating;

**2.** He has four long arms, beautiful shoulders, a handsome forehead, a pure smile, and ears that are decorated with shark-shaped earrings;

**3.** He has a darkish complexion;

**4.** He is dressed in golden-yellowish garments;

**5.** He has four arms- each holding a conch shell, disc, club, and lotus flower;

**6.** Around the neck is a garland of flowers;

**7.** He wears an effulgent golden crown;

**8.** The feet are decorated with ankle bells;

**9.** The arms are decorated with gem studded bracelets;

**10.** A golden belt girdles the waist.

# The Mystic Powers

Uddhava inquired, "Is it true that if a person diligently practices the meditation technique, you described, he will awaken the mystic powers within him?"

Krishna answered, "Absolutely. If a yogi diligently practices meditation by controlling his senses; conquering his breathing process; steadying his mind and fixing his awareness on me, then various mystic powers (**siddhis**) will be manifested from within him."

Uddhava asked, "How many types of siddhis are there, and what is the nature of each power?"

Krishna replied, "There are eight primary and ten secondary siddhis. Then there are five additional siddhis of yoga and meditation. Among these, eight originate from me; ten appear from the material mode of goodness and additional five are manifested from yoga and manifestation.

**The eight primary siddhis which originate from me are-**

**1. Anima-** The ability to become smaller than the smallest and go inside or through objects;

**2. Mahima-** Becoming greater than the greatest;

**3. Laghima-** Becoming lighter than the lightest;

**4. Garima-** Becoming heavier than the heaviest;

**5. Prapti-** Manifesting whatever one desires;

**6. Prakamya-** Experiencing any enjoyable object found in any part of the material universe;

**7. Ishita-** Power to create and control things;

**8. Vashita-** Controlling other living beings;

**The ten secondary siddhis are-**

**1. Anurmi-mattvam-** Not bothered by hunger, thirst, and other bodily disturbances;

**2. Dura-sravana-** Hearing distant sounds and conversations.

**3. Dura-darsanam-** Remote viewing;

**4. Manah-javah-** Travelling to any location instantly, just by thinking of the spot;

**5. Kama-rupam-** Changing into any shape or a being;

**6. Para-kaya pravesanam-** Entering anyone's body anytime you want;

**7. Svachanda mrityuh-** Choosing the time of your death;

**8. Devanam saha krida anudarsanam-** Witnessing the activities of beings in other realms or dimensions;

**9. Yatha sankalpa samsiddhih-** The power of intent;

**10. Ajna apratihata gatih-** Spoken words becoming a reality.

**The five siddhis of yoga and meditation are-**

**1. Trikala jnatvam-** Knowing the past, present and future;

**2. Advandvam-** Tolerance of heat, cold and other dualities;

**3. Para citta adi abhijnata-** Reading the minds of other living beings;

**4. Agni arka ambu viṣa adinam pratiṣṭambhaḥ-** Checking the influence of fire, sun, water, poison, and so on;

**5. Aparajayah-** Remaining undefeated by others."

# Awakening the Powers

Uddhava asked, "Lord, how are these siddhis attained?

Krishna said, "It takes a lot of practice, patience and perseverance to reach the siddha (mystic) stage. It's not an easy path to follow. A neophyte needs to diligently practice the yoga meditational technique to awaken the latent siddhis and become an adept."

Uddhava spoke, "Lord, Please tell me how the various powers are manifested."

Krishna answered, "How can I refuse you, my dearest friend? I will reveal the techniques for awakening the various powers. (See Powers1 to 23)

After listening about the yogic powers, Uddhava asked, "Are these powers desirable?"

Krishna answered, "These siddhis are actually obstacles on the path of self-realization. Most practitioners are tempted to use these powers for their material gain and forget the true purpose of meditation- eternal bliss.

No power in the material universe can ever equal the happiness one can attain by associating with me or remaining totally desireless.

**Why do you need siddhis if you have me?"**

(If you are interested, check out **"How to Be the Master of Mystic Yoga"** http://ASIN.cc/2BnNYZW**)**

# Power 1- Contraction

## Sanskrit Name: Anima

**Power:** The ability to become smaller than the smallest and go inside or through objects

"An adept needs to fix his mind on me in my sub-atomic form, which pervades all subtle elements and worship that form alone to attain **anima** siddhi."

# Power 2- Expansion

**Sanskrit Name: Mahima**

**Power:** Becoming greater than the greatest

"One who concentrates his mind on me as situated in the primordial matter as the Supersoul of the total material elements can attain **mahima** siddhi."

# Power 3- Lightness

### Sanskrit Name: Laghima

**Power:** Becoming lighter than the lightest

"By meditating on me as that which empowers the atoms of each of the **tattvas** (elements of creation) - earth, water, fire, wind and space, a yogi can attain **laghima** siddhi, which enables him to become as light as an atom."

# Power 4- Becoming Heavy

### Sanskrit Name: Garima

**Power:** The ability to become infinitely heavy

"Meditating on me as existing within everything and as the essence of the atomic constituents of material elements, one attains **garima** siddhi."

# Power 5- Manifestation

**Sanskrit Name: Prapti**

**Power:** Manifesting whatever one desires

"One who meditates on me as the element of false ego, generated from the mode of goodness, attains **prapti** siddhi."

# Power 6- Remote Sensing

## Sanskrit Name: Prakamya

**Power:** - Experiencing any enjoyable object found in any part of the material universe

"One who concentrates his mind on me as the Supersoul; the omnipresent thread of consciousness within all beings and who is beyond material perception, attains **prakamya** siddhi. By absorbing the mind in the existence of each material element, one can obtain their potencies."

# Power 7- Lordship

### Sanskrit Name: Ishita

**Power:** Controlling all the elements of universe and possessing absolute lordship.

"One who meditates on my form as Lord Vishnu, the Supersoul and the controller of the three modes of material nature, attains **ishita** siddhi."

# Power 8- Controlling Living Beings

### Sanskrit Name: Vashita

**Power:** Controlling other living beings

"One, who meditates on my form as the Supreme Lord, becomes endowed with my power and thus achieves **vashita** siddhi."

# Power 9- Control Body Functions

**Sanskrit Name: Anurmi-mattvam**

**Power:** - Not bothered by hunger, thirst, and other bodily disturbances

"One who fixes his mind on my form as the Lord of the mode of goodness and the upholder of religious principles attains **Anurmi-mattvam siddhi** which is freedom from- hunger, thirst, decay, death, grief, and illusion."

# Power 10- Clairaudience

### Sanskrit Name: Dura-sravana

**Power:** Hearing distant sounds and conversations

"If an adept meditates on me as the transcendent sound which vibrates through time and space, he attains **dura-sravana** siddhi."

# Power 11- Remote Viewing

**Sanskrit Name:** Dura-darsanam

**Power:** Remote viewing

"An adept who meditates on me as the sun that shines and the eye that sees and combines the light of both then he attains **dura-darsanam** siddhi or the power to see any distant thing."

# Power 12- Astral Travelling

## Sanskrit Name: Manah-javah

**Power:** Travelling to any location instantly, just by thinking of the spot

"When one completely absorbs his mind in me and meditates on me as the unifying force of body, breath and mind, he can attain the **manah-javah** that allows him to travel in a moment to anywhere he desires."

# Power 13- Shape Shifting

### Sanskrit Name: Kama-rupam

**Power:** Changing into any shape or a being

"When a yogi desires to assume a particular shape by focusing his mind in that way, that shape will appear before him. Such a mystic perfection called **kama-rupam** is possible by meditating upon me as the form that assumes all forms."

# Power 14- Psychically Enter Another Body

## Sanskrit Name: Para-kaya pravesanam

**Power:** Entering anyone's body anytime you want

"A yogi who desires to enter another body should meditate upon himself as being situated in that body. As easily as a bumblebee enters and leaves a flower, a yogi, with the help of his subtle body, can enter another body through the pathway of **prana** (life air)."

# Power15- Choosing Time of Death

## Sanskrit Name: Svachanda mrityuh

**Power:** Choosing the time of your death

"To achieve the mystic perfection called **svachanda mrityuh**, a yogi should block his anus with the heel of his foot and then gradually guide the prana, from the heart to the chest, then to the neck, and finally to the crown of the head called the **brahma-randhra**, the yogi then gives up his material body and guides the spirit soul to his desired destination."

# Power 16- Extraterrestrial Contacts

### Sanskrit Name: Devanam saha krida anudarsanam

**Power:** Witnessing the activities of beings in other realms or dimensions

"If one meditates upon the mode of purified goodness, which is situated within me, then he gets to enjoy life with the celestial nymphs who will descend from their heavenly realms."

# Power 17- Intent

**Sanskrit Name: Yatha sankalpa samsiddhih**

**Power:** The power of intent

"One who has absolute faith in me and thus concentrates his mind upon me, knowing that my will is always done, will have all his desires fulfilled."

# Power 18- The Power of the Spoken Word

**Sanskrit Name: Ajna apratihata gatih**

**Power:** Spoken words becoming a reality

"One who has merged with my self-contained Oneness, his spoken words will come true."

# Power 19- Precognition and Postcognition

## Sanskrit Name: Trikala jnatvam

**Power:** Knowing the past, present and future

"One who has become purified by constant devotion to me and controlled his mind by the practice of meditation, becomes cognizant of past, present, and future."

# Power 20- Physical Tolerance

### Sanskrit Name: Advandvam

**Power:** Tolerance of heat, cold and other dualities

"Just as the body of an aquatic animal cannot be injured by water, the body of a yogi, whose mind has completely calmed down by the process of the yogic meditational technique, can tolerate heat, cold and other dualities."

# Power 21- Telepathy

## Sanskrit Name: Para citta adi abhijnata

**Power:** Reading the minds of other living beings

"One who has become purified by constant devotion to me and controlled his mind by the practice of meditation will be able to read the thoughts of other living beings."

# Power 22- Immunity

**Sanskrit Name:** Agni arka ambu viṣa adinam pratiṣṭambhaḥ

**Power:** Checking the influence of fire, sun, water, poison, and so on

"The body of a yogi, whose mind has completely calmed down by the process of the yogic meditational technique, cannot be injured by fire, the sun, water, poison, and so forth."

# Power 23- Invincibility

**Sanskrit Name: Aparajayah**

**Power:** Remaining undefeated by others

"A yogi, who constantly meditates on my form which holds various weapons in their hands, cannot be conquered by anyone."

# Divine Attributes

Uddhava asked, "Please tell me about your divine attributes by which you pervade the universe and abide in them. How do I contemplate you, O blessed Lord?"

Krishna remembered Arjuna and smiled, "Dear Uddhava, what's the need to know all this? My other great devotee, the **Pandava** prince **Arjuna**, had also asked me the same question on the battlefield of **Kurukshetra**.

I will tell you what I told him-

- I am the beginning, middle, and end of creation;
- I am the father and mother of this universe, and its entire support;
- I support the entire cosmos with only a fragment of my being;
- The birth and dissolution of the cosmos itself take place in me. There is nothing that exists separate from me. The entire universe is suspended from me as my necklace of jewels;

- I am time, the destroyer of all;
- I am the supreme poet, the first cause, the sovereign ruler, subtler than the tiniest particle, the support of all, inconceivable, bright as the sun, beyond darkness;
- All the scriptures lead to me; I am their author and their wisdom;
- I am heat; I give and withhold the rain. I am immortality and I am death; I am what is and what is not;
- I am the taste of pure water and the radiance of the sun, moon and other heavenly bodies;
- I am the sacred word and the sound heard in air, and the courage of human beings;
- I am the ritual and the sacrifice; I am the offering and the fire which consumes it, and the one to whom it is offered;
- I am the sweet fragrance in the earth and the radiance of fire;
- I am the life in every creature and the striving of the spiritual aspirant;

- I enter breathing creatures and dwell within as the life-giving breath. I am the fire in the stomach which digests all food;
- My eternal seed is found in every creature;
- I am the power of discrimination in those who are intelligent, and the glory of the noble. In those who are strong, I am strength, free from passion and selfish attachment;
- I am desire itself, if that desire is in harmony with the purpose of life;
- I am the friend of all creatures, the Lord of the universe, the end of all offerings and all spiritual disciplines;
- I am the sum of all knowledge, the purifier, the syllable Om; I am the sacred scriptures;
- I am the goal of life, the Lord and support of all, the inner witness, the abode of all. I am the only refuge, the one true friend of my believers;
- I am ever present to those who have realized me in every creature. Seeing all life as my

manifestation, they are never separated from me.

## Bheeshma Teaches Self-Realization

Krishna continued, "If you have understood the illusory nature of the material universe, then there is no need for further speculation about the laws of the universe.

If you have achieved perfection by studying the scriptures and by yogic meditation, then you will know that living with me in the Universal Consciousness should be the supreme goal of life. Performing austerities, offering prayers, visiting temples and places of worship, giving charity, or engaging in pious activities will not give the same result as introspection about yourself.

In ancient times, great sages worshiped me as the Lord of all sacrifice and the Supersoul in everyone's heart and achieved salvation.

The soul, hidden behind the mind, wrongly identifies the physical body as real even though it is illusory and has no real existence. The physical body also undergoes various transformations from birth till death and then ceases to exist.

The soul is immortal and never changes. You must, therefore, think of the body as a temporary manifestation of the illusory energy of the Lord."

Uddhava prayed, "O Lord! Please instruct me how to detach from all material objects and perceive the true reality of existence."

Krishna answered, "Did you know the eldest Pandava, King Yudhisthira, asked the same question, regarding the path of liberation, to the revered grandsire, Bheeshma, who lay gravely wounded on the battlefield of Kurukshetra?

Listen to what Bheeshma instructed Yudhisthira-

"Dear Yudhisthira, I am glad that you are interested to know about liberation. With Lord Krishna's blessings, I will tell you what I know-

- There is a combination of three, five, nine or eleven elements in all living beings and ultimately one supreme element within all twenty-eight;
- If you look beyond the twenty-eight material elements, and see the Supersoul, from whom these elements have emanated, your

knowledge is called "**vijnana**" or **self-realized knowledge**;

- All matter in the illusory universe undergoes three stages— **creation, existence** and **destruction**. They are the stages of material causation. That which consistently accompanies all these three stages and remains unaffected when these stages are annihilated is called "**sat**," or **eternal existence**;
- One can figure out the illusory nature of the material world, through various sources, and become detached from the dualities of material existence;
- One should understand that everything has a beginning and an end in this material universe and learn to be detached from objects that tempt the senses;
- If you understand that nothing is permanent in this illusory universe and the only reality is the Supersoul and the immortal soul residing within all living beings, you will start seeing everything in relation to the Supersoul."

## Q & A Session

Uddhava spoke, "My dear Lord Krishna, my mind is brimming with questions. They are-

**1.** How many types of disciplinary regulations and prohibitions there are?

**2.** What are mental equilibrium, self-control, tolerance and steadfastness?

**3.** What are charity, austerity, heroism, truth and reality?

**4.** What is renunciation, and what is real wealth?

**5.** What is religious remuneration and what is the greatest strength?

**6.** What is opulence and what is the reward of life?

**7.** What are the best education, humility and real beauty?

**8.** What are happiness and misery?

**9.** Who is learned, and who is a fool?

**10.** What are the true and the false paths in life?

**11.** What are heaven and hell?

**12.** Who is a true friend, and what are one's temporary and real homes?

**13.** Define a rich man and a poor man.

**14.** Who is a miser and who are the controller and slave?"

Krishna laughed, "Wow, Uddhava! These are a bag full of questions!

I will strive to answer them—

**1. Types of disciplinary regulations and prohibitions-**

Nonviolence, honesty, not coveting others' property, desirelessness, humility, not possessive, religious, celibacy, silence, steadiness, forgiveness, and fearlessness—these twelve are referred to as **yama**.

Personal hygiene, purity of inner body and mind, chanting the holy names of the Lord, worshiping me, austerity, holy rituals, faith, serving guests, visiting places of worship and pilgrimage, engaging in activities prescribed by the spiritual master—these twelve are called **niyama**.

These twenty-four practices bestow all desired benedictions upon those who devotedly cultivate them.

**2. Mental equilibrium, self-control, tolerance and steadfastness-**

Focusing the mind on me totally constitutes **mental equilibrium**, and having complete control of the senses is **self-control**. **Tolerance** means patiently enduring miserable situations, and controlling the urges of the tongue and genitals is **steadfastness**.

**3. Charity, austerity, heroism, truth and reality-**

**Charity** is not to envy others. Abstaining from sense gratification is **austerity**. **Heroism** is suppressing one's natural tendency to enjoy material benefits. Truth means to speak and behave honestly with others. **Reality** is seeing the Supersoul in everything and everything in the Supersoul.

**4. Renunciation and real wealth-**

**Renunciation** means detachment from material activities. **Real wealth** is belief and faith in the Supreme Lord.

**5. Religious remuneration and greatest strength-**

**Religious remuneration** is being a devoted student of a spiritual guru with the desire to acquire real knowledge, and the **greatest strength** is the yogic meditation technique.

### 6. Opulence and reward of life-

Those who possess these six qualities- immense strength, fame, wealth, knowledge, beauty, and renunciation, can be termed as **opulent**. **Opulence** is my own nature, in which I exhibit the above six qualities in abundance. The ultimate **reward** of life is devotional service unto me.

### 7. Best education, humility and real beauty-

The **best education** is to remove the conception of duality from the mind of the conditioned soul. **Real modesty** is being humble and attributing all your activities to the Lord. **Real beauty** means possessing good qualities, such as desirelessness.

### 8. Happiness and misery-

**Real happiness** is to be detached from worldly attachments, whereas **misery** means the results of sex addiction.

### 9. Learned and fool-

A **learned** person is one who knows how to be liberated from the Game of Life, and a **fool** is one whose mind has trapped him into body consciousness.

### 10. The true and the false paths in life-

The **true path** is the path of self-realization that ultimately leads to me. The **false path** is the path where you get tempted by worldly pleasures and forget your true purpose of life.

**11. Heaven and hell-**

**Heaven** is the predominance of the mode of goodness. **Hell** is the predominance of the mode of ignorance.

**12. A true friend and one's temporary / permanent homes-**

I am the **true friend** of my devotees because I never let them down. The physical body is **the temporary home** of the soul whereas the **permanent abode** is with me.

**13. A rich man and a poor man-**

A person who is an optimist and has all good qualities can be termed **rich**. A person who is a pessimist and dissatisfied with life is a **poor** person.

**14. Miser, controller and slave-**

A **miser** is a person who cannot control his senses. A person who is detached from worldly pleasures can be termed a **controller**. A person who is attached to worldly pleasures is a **slave**.

My dear Uddhava, does that make sense?

I guess there is no need for further discussions of the good and the bad because to constantly differentiate between good and bad is itself a bad thing. The best way out is to go beyond material good and evil and be totally detached from such dualities."

## Path of Devotion

Uddhava inquired, "My dear Lord, the Vedic literature classifies the different types of activities-pious and impious and heaven for the virtuous and hell for the sinners.

Lord, without making distinctions between virtue and sin, how can one figure out your instructions, (in the form of the Vedic literature), which orders one to act virtuously and forbids one to act sinfully?"

Krishna answered, "Dear Uddhava, I created three paths of advancement—**jnana yoga, karma yoga,** and **bhakti yoga** for the benefit of humans.

**Jnana yoga** or the path of knowledge is recommended for those who want to become detached from the temptations of worldly pleasures.

**Karma yoga** or the path of action is recommended for those who are fond of worldly pleasures and ignorant of the miseries that accompany them.

**Bhakti yoga** or the path of devotion is recommended for those who are not very disgusted or attached to material life.

If an individual is not comfortable with the three paths of advancement then he must act according to the regulative principles prescribed by the Vedic literature.

If an individual carries out his worldly duties without expectation of results, worships the Lord as per prescribed religious guidelines and avoids forbidden activities, then he doesn't need to spend time in heaven or hell. Such a person is also able to attain divine knowledge.

Divine knowledge is beyond the grasp of inhabitants of the heavenly or the hellish planets. It is possible for only humans. So, a sensible person should not waste his precious human existence and aspire to live in the heavenly or the hellish planets. However, since the human body is mortal, one should sincerely endeavor to attain the perfection of life before death arrives.

A soul needs to be very lucky to play a human role in the Game of Life. The human body is like a sailboat.

Its helmsman is a spiritual guru who can guide you along the path of salvation and my teachings are the favorable winds. If the soul does not utilize its human role for crossing over the ocean of material existence it will be a loser in the Game of Life.

If an individual becomes disgruntled after many attempts at worldly success, he is liable to be disgusted with worldly attachments and becomes detached. This should not be a temporary phase. The individual should fix the mind in self-realization and not allow the mind to deviate from this path, as it is wont to do.

One should control the mind like a **horse trainer**. A trainer, who trains wild horses, will first allow the horse some freedom. Then, by pulling the ropes tied to its neck, he will gradually control the horse. Likewise, the mind cannot be subjugated initially. It must be gradually trained so that it eventually sticks to the path of self-realization.

The aspirant should observe the temporary nature of all material objects and its cycle of creation, existence and destruction.

If he becomes disgusted with the temporary, illusory nature of this universe, he will become detached and gradually stop the false identification with matter.

If a yogi commits an offence due to carelessness, he should neutralize the karmic reaction by continuing with his yogic meditation techniques. He need not undergo severe penance or adopt any other method to purify himself.

If an aspirant understands the diligent observance of his practice constitutes piety, and the neglect of his spiritual practices constitutes sin, then he should endeavor to become detached by earnestly following his discipline.

My devotee should be content and worship me with great faith and belief. Even though he engages in worldly pursuits he will always remember that such activities simply lead to misery, and so he sincerely repents such activities.

Whatever can be attained by other scriptural procedures, my devotees can easily attain that.

If my devotee desires liberation from the Game of Life or wants to live in the heavenly planets, he can achieve these without difficulty.

However, pure devotees are not allured by my offer of liberation from the Game of Life and they reject it. Such devotees are not subject to pious and impious actions. They have become perfectly desireless.

Those who follow the path of devotional service are detached from all worldly illusions and attain salvation."

## Miser Who Became a Tramp

Krishna continued, "Dear Uddhava, harsh words, especially spoken by jerks, can be very painful. Even a sharp object piercing the skin would be less painful. Highly evolved persons also get shaken if somebody hurls a barrage of insults at them.

A devotee who actually desires to attain perfection in this very life should tolerate all kinds of mistreatment at the hands of wicked people. He should ignore these obstructions and focus his mind in devotional service and remain undisturbed.

Let me narrate you the parable of a miser who became a tramp-

In the kingdom of **Avanti**, there lived a **Brahman** (priestly class) who was very rich. He was also miserly, lusty, greedy, and had anger issues.

He treated his family members and guests with utter contempt. Everybody hated him- his wife, children, relatives and even his servants. They were so disgusted by him that they openly showed their hatred towards him.

He did not pray, nor conduct any rituals to please the demigods, who had made him wealthy, and they, too, were angry at his attitude. They decided to take all his wealth back. As a result, the Brahman started making huge losses in his business venture; some of his relatives cheated on him; thieves robbed him; the king's men confiscated his property for not paying taxes and, thus, he lost it all. His family members left him and he was all alone and spooked. He pondered over his misfortune for a long time and figured out that he could do nothing to alleviate his condition. As a result, he became strangely detached.

The Brahman thought out aloud-

"O what a loser I was! I made a lot of money and did not spend a dime on myself, my family or used it for religious / charitable purposes. It's the law of wealth. If you hoard it like a miser you will never be happy because you are worried of losing it all. If, by misfortune, they lose their wealth (like me) they are perplexed. Nobody loves a miser or a loser. After death, such miserly souls go to the hellish planets and live in utter hell there.

Wealth attracts many undesirables—theft, violence, falsehood, sharks, arrogance, conflicts, jealousy, competition, enmity, vices, sex addiction, gambling and intoxication. Attachment to excessive wealth is the beginning of all troubles!

Even a man's relatives and friends, who apparently loved him, have been known to break off the relationships and become enemies due to a dispute over a tiny sum of money. Some of them are even willing to kill to get what they think is rightfully theirs.

Playing the role of a human, in the Game of Life, is the gateway to ultimate salvation. Why do we forget this truth and become attached to the accumulation of wealth, which brings with it all kinds of problems?

One who does not share his good fortune with the demigods and other living beings will certainly come crashing down. Look at me. I did none of these things and wasted my life. Now that I have become an old man, it is too late for me to do anything worthwhile.

Why should a person suffer because of his useless efforts to accumulate wealth?

Is it due to forces beyond his control? Nobody's permanent in this world. So, why waste your finite life span in foolish accumulation of wealth?

I sense that the Supreme Soul must have been pleased with me because he gave me this suffering which made me detached. This detached feeling is the boat that will carry me across the ocean of material existence.

Hopefully, if I have some more time to live, then I will perform austerities while subsisting upon the bare minimum of food. I will also take a vow of silence as foolish talk will just waste my time."

Having conditioned his mind in this way, the Brahman slashed the knots of material attachment within his heart and decided to become a tramp.

The Brahman went from place to place, carefully controlling his senses, mind, and intelligence. He begged for food and alms and subsided on them. He never revealed his true spiritual position so that he was not recognized by others.

He became free from all bad association by remaining aloof from those who hankered after worldly pleasures.

However, he attracted the attention of vagrants who taunted and insulted him with many harsh words. These miscreants snatched most of his belongings. Sometimes they pretended to return these things, only to snatch it back again.

When the Brahman sat on the river bank to eat the food that he collected by begging, evil persons would appear from nowhere and throw dirt over his food or spit on him.

Some scoundrels figured that he had taken a vow of silence, and tried to make him speak. If he did not reply, they would beat him with sticks. There were others who tormented by calling him a thief, hypocrite, loser and a cheat. Others called him a con man who had become a tramp to fill his belly.

In this way, the Brahman repeatedly suffered the humiliation in peace and he remained steadfast in his determination.

Keeping himself fixed in the mode of goodness, he began singing this song-

"Nobody is responsible for my happiness and distress. Not the miscreants, demigods, my body, destiny or time.

The true culprit is the mind that causes happiness and distress and binds our soul to the Game of Life. The mind manifests the functions of the modes of nature, from which evolve the activities of the modes of goodness, passion, and ignorance. From the interaction of the modes of nature, the various species of life evolve.

Although the Supersoul is present with me in this body, he is not involved with my actions because he is not affected by the three modes, and thus does not identify with the physical body and mind. He is simply a well-wisher, and a neutral observer.

On the other hand, I, the soul, has foolishly associated the mind, which is like a mirror reflecting external reality, as my very Self. The mind has lured me into enjoying the worldly pleasures, under the dictation of the three modes of material nature.

Performing charity; adhering to prescribed duties; reading or listening to the Holy Scriptures; pious actions and purifying vows all help to subdue the mind. Indeed, **concentration of the mind on the Supersoul is the goal of yoga.** If one's mind is controlled, what is the need for performing all the said activities?

Even the demigods, who control the senses of the conditioned souls, are controlled by their minds, but the mind cannot be controlled by anyone, because it is immensely powerful. If anyone is able to control his mind, he will become the master of the universe.

Those who fail to conquer their minds suffer from intolerable urges and are tormented by them. They become agitated, pick quarrels with others, blinded by their perceptions that other people are either their friends, enemies, or indifferent to them.

Individuals who identify with the physical body, which is a product of the mind, foolishly think in terms of "I" and "mine" and wander in endless darkness.

If the miscreants caused my suffering, then what happened to my inner self? Happiness and misery, which are the results of the contact of the senses with the material objects, do not affect the soul. If you hurt yourself then whom do you blame for your pain? You or the demigods?

If the soul is considered the cause of happiness and distress, then there is no reason to be angry about it, because happiness and distress would be the nature of the soul. It is said, nothing exists besides our-self. If one perceives something else besides the inner self, then that must be considered an illusion. Therefore, why be angry?

Astrology stipulates the planets are the cause of happiness and distress, then where is the relationship with the inner self? If astrology is to be believed, then the planets can only cause happiness or distress for that which has taken birth. However, the soul is birthless and distinct from the material body and the planets. Then, against whom should he direct his anger?

The body has no life and hence, it cannot be the actual recipient of happiness and distress, nor can the soul, which is distinct from the physical body. Then, at whom can one become angry?

The false ego, which manifests the visible material creation, is subjected to happiness and distress. The soul can never be affected by happiness and distress by any being or incidents, anywhere, any place or any time.

When one realizes this fact, he will no longer have any fear of any material condition. I shall walk the path of self-realization by becoming a devotee of the Supreme Lord."

After this enlightenment, the Brahman was a changed person. He remained fixed in his duty and chanted this song, whenever he was troubled by people or circumstances. He transcended the dualities of material happiness and distress and achieved eternal bliss."

# Folly of King Puruvara

Krishna continued, "If an individual sees the results of the three modes of nature as illusion, he avoids being influenced by them, although constantly surrounded by them. He does not accept them as ultimate reality because he has figured out the modes of nature and their results are not perpetual facts.

Let me tell you the story of **King Puruvara**-

There was a king named Puruvara. He had married a celestial beauty named **Urvashi**. He enjoyed sex with her for many years but was never satiated. He wanted to make love to her the whole day. Urvashi got tired of it and decided to leave for her celestial abode. At that time, the king was sleeping naked on his bed after making love to her.

When he realized that Urvashi had left his palace, even though he was naked, he ran after her like a crazy, besotted fool, crying out, "Darling! Don't leave me." She did not heed his impassioned pleas.

He lamented, "Alas! Just see what a sucker I was! I got enthralled by her embraces and lost my senses.

What a waste of time on such foolish pursuits! Imagine, a powerful king being totally captivated by a woman!"

He continued, "Although I am a mighty emperor, that woman hardly cared and left me as if I was no better than a blade of grass. Without shame and naked, I cried out like a madman while following her. I acted like an ass in heat that got kicked by its mate for trying to force itself on her!

Shame on me! I totally forgot myself, although I considered myself to be a very intelligent person. I was no better than an animal.

I have lost count of the number of times I made love to her and kissed her sweet lips but I was never satisfied just like a fire, which is never extinguished if you continually pour oil into its flames.

Who can save me from this pitiable condition?

Only the Supreme Lord, who exists beyond the purview of the material senses, will be able to redeem my fallen soul. Therefore, I shall now devote my time to worshiping the Supreme Personality of Godhead.

Urvashi warned me many times about my excesses but I fail to take notice of it. So, how can I blame her for my predicament when it is I who acted out of ignorance? I did not control my senses, and so I am like an ignorant person who mistakes a rope for a snake.

I was attracted by a woman's beauty and fragrance, forgetting that these are simply coverings of a destructible body. I was totally disillusioned.

Do we know who owns our body? Does it belong to the parents, who helped create it? Does it belong to one's spouse, who gives it pleasure? Is it the property of the state? Does it belong to the funeral pyre, or to the animals that may one day devour it? Does it belong to the Self who experiences its pleasures and pains, or does it belong to our friends and relatives, who love us?

Thus, we are not sure who is the real owner of the body but one certainly becomes very attached to it.

Although the physical body is destined to turn into dust after death, a man gazing at the face of a beautiful woman wistfully thinks, "Wow! She is very attractive! What a figure she has, and how beautiful is her smile!"

What difference is there between lowly creatures and those who take pleasure in the material body, which is composed of skin, flesh, blood, nerves, pus, bone, marrow, stool and urine?

After carefully pondering over this gross subject, one should neither associate with women, or sex-addicted persons. After all, as soon as there is contact between the senses and their objects, the mind is sure to become agitated. Therefore, one should not let his senses associate with such people. Even self-controlled persons are wary of the six enemies of the mind- **lust, anger, intoxication, illusion, envy** and **fear.** Tell this to a foolish person like me."

Krishna concluded, "After mulling over this, King Puruvara became a self-realized person and finally achieved peace.

An intelligent person should therefore stop associating with people who will lead him astray and interact only with saintly devotees, whose discussions can help dilute the mind's attachment to worldly objects.

My devotees fix their minds on me, and do not depend upon other sources of enjoyment. They are always peaceful, compassionate, humble, loving, detached and self-realized."

## The Soul and the Body

Uddhava inquired, "Lord, who actually experiences this material existence- the soul which is innately endowed with perfect knowledge or the body, which is not a conscious entity?

Krishna answered, "As long as the ignorant soul identifies itself with its physical body and worldly attachments, it will live a meaningless, illusory material existence. The living entities propensity for worldly success leads to all sorts of inconveniences.

A person experiences many undesirable things in his dream, but upon awakening, he is no longer troubled by such dreams, even though he may remember them. Likewise, happiness, sadness, fear, anger, greed, delusion, and lust are experiences of the false ego and not of the soul. The soul should not be affected by these experiences and think of them as illusory.

The soul plays a role in the Game of Life, as per its karmic actions and due to ignorance, it identifies with its body and mind. In this way, it becomes subject to the happiness and miseries of the physical world.

If the soul wants to opt out of this Game of Life then it should cut off its false identification with the physical world and live within this world free from material attachment.

The material body, which is predominantly made of matter and endowed with the senses, intelligence, ego, sense objects is not the soul. It does not experience material existence."

Uddhava asked, "What should a neophyte do if his physical and mental body develops problems which obstruct his spiritual progress?"

Krishna replied, "If a neophyte's body is afflicted by various disturbances, such as disease, the following process is recommended-

- Hot and cold sensations can be counteracted by meditating on the sun and moon;
- Gastric disorders can be controlled by proper diet and by practicing sitting postures and breath control;
- Inauspicious planetary positions, fear of snakebite etc., can be counteracted by proper

medicinal treatment, rituals, penance, chanting of mantras, and so on;

- If a neophyte has lust problems, then he should continually think of me and chant my name whenever such thoughts come up;
- One can destroy the obstructions of pride and false ego by following the methods of the mystic masters;
- Yogis practice the yogic techniques to remain forever youthful. A true devotee is not impressed by such techniques and shuns such practices because he knows the soul, like a tree, is permanent, and the body, like the tree's fruit, is perishable.

My true devotees don't need to hanker after body perfections because they have figured out their true self and the source of unlimited happiness."

# Bhakti Yoga

Uddhava spoke, "O Lord, apparently the yogic meditation technique might be very difficult for ordinary persons who are not self-controlled or have patience to practice it. Therefore, please tell me a simpler way how one can easily attain perfection."

Krishna answered, "Sure, Uddhava! I shall describe to you the religious principles of devotion which human beings can imbibe and conquer death.

You can start by always remembering me and performing your devotional and daily duties without hesitation. If it is possible, you should reside in a holy place that is inhabited by other devotees of mine, and interact with them. I am pleased when my devotees sing or discuss my activities, and take part in rituals / festivals dedicated to me.

You should see me as being situated within your Self as well as within the hearts of all living entities. A person, who believes that I am present in all living beings, whether he is a priest or a thief, is considered to be a wise person.

Jealousy, anger, envy, ego do not affect the one who constantly meditates on me as being situated within all living entities.

People might start ridiculing you if you talk about abandoning body consciousness or if you tell them that I am situated in all living beings. Ignore them and pity them for their foolishness.

You should utilize your mind, words, and bodily functions for realizing my presence within all living entities. I consider this to be the best method of spiritual enlightenment. A devotee has nothing to lose and everything to gain if he believes in the omnipresence of the Lord.

Don't you lament if you suffer a loss? Is crying not a useless emotion under the circumstances? Will you recoup your loss if you cry? However, if you exhibit any useless emotions while engaging in devotional service to me, it carries weight with me. I care!

Does this make sense?

Let me say this- Anyone who properly understands this knowledge will be doubt-free and attain self-realization."

Uddhava spoke, "I get it, Lord. Everything's crystal clear. Now, kindly tell me how family guys can attain salvation by the execution of their prescribed duties."

Krishna smiled, "I am pleased with your inquiry. Listen-

- A family guy should study the religious scriptures; worship the saints; remember his forefathers; worship the demigods by rituals; take care of fellow human beings and help animals by offering them food, water and shelter, if possible;
- A family guy should maintain his dependents with his inherited wealth and honest earnings. He should also utilize his wealth for religious and charitable purposes;
- He should not become unduly attached to his family or wealth and remember these are illusory and temporary in nature. He should remain at home just like a guest and not get entangled by domestic affairs;

- A family guy devotee who faithfully worships me by the performance of his duties can live in his home or at a holy place of pilgrimage. If he has grownup children and he has no interest for material enjoyment, he should lead a secluded, retired life in prayer and devotion;
- However, if a family guy has strong desires to enjoy his wealth; have sex with his wife and have fun with his family, friends and relatives; thinking that these phases will last forever is in the densest darkness of ignorance.

Thus, as a result of his foolish behavior, a family guy who gets attached to his family lives a distressed life, forever.

**Remember the parable of the Dove family?"**

Uddhava answered, "I will always remember the parable of the Dove family! There's an awesome message in your words- Love and take care of your family but don't be strongly attached or you will be miserable. Now, please help clear up this doubt. Should a devotee try to impose this divine knowledge on non-believers?"

Krishna answered, "No! Do not try to impose this knowledge on anyone who is a skeptic; persons who will ridicule you; non-devotees; or arrogant or egotistic persons.

This knowledge should be taught to only genuine believers, devotees or persons who thirst for spiritual wisdom.

People try to succeed in life by means of their efforts, by good luck, knowledge and other methods. A true devotee does not need to hanker after these worldly achievements. He can very easily find true success by associating with me. He achieves liberation from birth and death and experiences eternal bliss."

# Samkhya Philosophy

Krishna continued, "My dear Uddhava, I shall now describe to you the philosophy of **Samkhya**, which was propounded by sage **Kapila**.

By understanding this philosophy, you will be able to renounce all desires for material happiness, which ultimately result in distress.

The Supreme Lord manifested himself into two attributes— Primordial matter and the souls who want to enjoy the material things in the universe.

Of the two manifestations, one is the primordial matter, which comprises of the subtle causes and the products of matter and the other is the living being who considers himself an enjoyer of what the universe has on offer. To fulfill the desires of the living beings, I manifested the three material modes of nature- **goodness, passion** and **ignorance**.

From these modes, the first transformation that takes place is the physical universe. Then, the false ego, which befuddles the living beings' mind, originated.

False ego, which is comprised of matter and spirit, manifests in three categories- **Vaikarika** or the neutral stage of creation arising from the mode of goodness, **Tejas** or the initiative of creation arising from the mode of passion and **Tamas** the full display of material creation under the mode of ignorance. The five sense objects, the senses, and the mind are creations of the false ego.

From false ego in the mode of ignorance, **Tamasa**, the five objects of perception and the five gross elements were generated. From false ego in the mode of passion, **Rajasa**, the ten senses were generated, and from false ego in the mode of goodness, **Sattvika**, arose the eleven demigods who control the senses and the mind. At my command, all the elements combine to form the **universal egg**. Everything originates from this universal egg by the coordinated combination of the five gross elements. The souls, led by their minds, then start playing roles in the different worlds of the universe. Thus the physical universe contains both the material nature and its enjoyer, the soul.

Originally, the three modes of material nature exist in a state of equilibrium. The agitation of these modes leads to the creation, maintenance, and dissolution of the universe. Such events occur within the external energy of the Lord, and do not pertain to the souls.

As long as the Supersoul continues to glance upon material nature, the universe will continue to exist for the souls who want to play roles in it.

At the time of annihilation of the universe, all matter and energy merges into one another and the modes of nature merge with the unmanifest nature and the unmanifest merges into time. Time then merges into the Supersoul. Thus, the Supersoul remains alone after the dissolution of the universe.

When the sun rises, darkness hides. Likewise, when you understand the creation and the dissolution of the universe, the illusory conceptions of duality vanishes from the mind of the transcendentalist. Even if such thoughts enter his mind, it will not remain for long.

So, dear Uddhava, this is Samkhya philosophy which explains the theory of creation and annihilation."

# The Philosopher's Score

Uddhava inquired, "O Master, You said that there are twenty-eight elements: the Supersoul, the individual souls, primordial matter, false ego, the five gross elements, the five working senses, the five cognitive senses, the mind, the five sense objects, and the three modes of nature.

However, different philosophers seem to have different figures. Some say there are twenty-six elements, while still others point out twenty-five, seven, nine, six, four, or eleven elements, and even others who say that there are seventeen, sixteen, or thirteen. It doesn't add up. How is it that these philosophers categorize the material elements in different ways?

Please describe to me so that I may correctly figure this out."

Krishna spoke, "Each thinker has his own way of perceiving the material creation and since the subtle and gross material elements are situated within one another, various philosophers have arrived at different figures.

However, for those who have connected with me and who have controlled their senses, the differences of perception disappear and the very cause for argument is removed.

The subtle material elements are present within their transformations- the gross elements and the gross material elements that are present in their subtle causes. This is true because creation is enacted from subtle to gross in a series of transformations. For this reason, all the material elements are present in each element.

Therefore, regardless of the particular philosopher and his means of calculation, whether he includes material elements within their previous subtle causes or subsequent manifest products, I accept their conclusions as authoritative because a logical explanation can always be given for all such theories.

Knowledge is the feature of the mode of goodness, activities are the features of the mode of passion, and ignorance is the feature of the mode of ignorance.

Time is the product of the agitation of these three modes and the sum total of the conditioned souls' propensities is incorporated within the physical universe.

The nine basic truths are the spirit soul, nature, primordial matter, false ego, sky, air, fire, water, and earth. The ears, skin, eyes, nose, and tongue are the five knowledge-acquiring senses. The speech, hands, legs, anus, and genitals are the five working senses. The mind belongs to both these categories. Sound, touch, form, taste and smell are the objects of the cognitive senses. By their transformation, the five gross material elements are created. Movement, speech, propagation and excretion are functions of the working senses.

In the beginning of creation, the material elements, aided by the three modes, take form as the embodiment of all subtle causes and gross manifestations. The material elements then undergo transformations to manifest the universal egg.

Some philosophers opine there are seven elements—earth, water, fire, air, and ether, soul and the Supersoul, who is the basis of both the material elements and the individual souls. According to them, everything is produced from these seven elements.

Other thinkers disagree and say there are six elements-the Supersoul and the five gross material elements. According to them, the Supersoul has created the universe with the help of the elements that he had emanated from within him and then entered it.

Then there are those who say that there are four elements and the first element, the Self is the creator of the remaining three elements- fire, water, and earth. After manifesting, these elements combine to form the universe.

Some calculate the existence of seventeen basic elements—the five gross material elements, the five sense objects, the five senses, the mind, and the Self.

Philosophers that identify sixteen elements differ from the above observation because they have identified the Self with the mind.

Others conclude thirteen elements—the five gross elements, the five senses, the mind, the soul, and the Supreme Soul.

Some thinkers say there are eleven basic truths—the five gross elements, the five senses, and the soul.

There are others who believe in nine basic truths—the five gross elements, the mind, intelligence, false ego, and the soul.

Thus, philosophers have categorized the material elements in various ways."

## The Three Modes of Nature

Uddhava asked, "Lord, please tell me about the three modes of nature and how the conditioned soul is awarded his particular nature due to the association of the three modes of material nature."

Krishna spoke, "Sure. As you know there are three modes of nature- **goodness, passion** and **ignorance**.

**The qualities of the mode of goodness are-** Serenity, faith, modesty, self-control, tolerance, the power of discrimination, truthfulness, compassion, punctuality, renunciation, desirelessness, giving charity, and self-satisfaction.

**The qualities of the mode of passion are-** Lust, ambition, pride, thirst for life, false ego, gaining wealth through rituals and other techniques, discriminatory nature sense gratification, ready to fight, superiority complex, flatterer, belittling, bragger, and justifying one's actions by forceful methods.

**The qualities of the mode of ignorance are-** Anger, greed, falsehood, violence, envy, hypocrisy, fatigue syndrome, fight, complainer, idle dreamer, depression, poverty, fear, and procrastination.

Now hear about the combination of these three modes.

All these combinations manifest the mentality of "I" and "mine," which is present in all conditioned souls. The activities performed in this universe are also derived from the combination of the modes of material nature. If a person chooses to be a priest or a millionaire or anything else, his choice is due to his mind's interactions with the three modes of nature.

The three modes of material nature instigate the mind and soul to become attached to their physical bodies and material pleasures, causing them to continue playing roles in the Game of Life.

Let's check out how individuals behave in the various modes-

**Mode of goodness-**

- A person who is self-controlled and devoted can be understood to be predominantly in the mode of goodness;
- If the mode of goodness influences a person more than the other two modes, then he gets

bestowed with happiness, knowledge, piety, and other good qualities;

- One becomes fearless, alert and remains detached from the workings of the material mind;
- Such individuals, after death, get to live in the higher planets;
- A person in the mode of goodness carries out his worldly duties without attachment to the result;
- Knowledge of the distinction between real and unreal is in the mode of goodness;
- Residence in a holy place or forest is in the mode of goodness;
- Desirelessness is in the mode of goodness;
- Belief in the existence of the eternal self is in the mode of goodness;
- Fresh and healthy food obtained without difficulty is in the mode of goodness;
- Leading a happy and satisfied life is in the mode of goodness.

**Mode of passion-**

- A lustful person can be understood to be predominantly in the mode of passion;
- If the mode of passion influences a person more than the other two modes, then such a person always hankers after wealth and fame;
- Such persons have great attachment to material and sensual desires; have health and sleep problems due their over ambitious natures; have dreams and they are forever disturbed about their performance and their competition;
- These people continue to play various roles in the Game of Life;
- Work performed with the desire to enjoy the results is in the mode of passion;
- Knowledge based on worldly matters is in the mode of passion;
- Living in a town, city is in the mode of passion;
- A possessive person is said to be in the mode of passion;
- Belief that one should win the race, in the Game of Life, is in the mode of passion;

- Tasty and aphrodisiacal food is in the mode of passion;
- Happiness got from sense gratification is in the mode of passion.

**Mode of ignorance-**

- A person with anger management problems ignorance is recognized to be predominantly in the mode of ignorance;
- If the mode of ignorance influences a person more than the other two modes, then such a person only day-dreams, procrastinates, exhibits depressive and violent tendencies and becomes a loser in the game;
- These people take birth in lower species of living beings;
- Violent and criminal activities compelled by envy, lust or greed are in the mode of ignorance;
- Knowledge that does not increase one's awareness or makes you more ignorant is in the mode of ignorance;

- Residence in a vice-den or seedy places is in the mode of ignorance;
- A person who does not know what is to be done and what is not to be done is in the mode of ignorance;
- Propensity for sinful activities is in the mode of ignorance;
- Stale, unhealthy foods that cause distress, diseases and sickness are in the mode of ignorance;
- Happiness derived from sinful activities is in the mode of ignorance.

Thus, Uddhava, all these qualities, activities and objects are based on the three material modes of nature.

**Those who are free from the influence of the three modes of material nature, attain salvation."**

Uddhava inquired, "What are the qualities of people in the mode of transcendence?"

Krishna answered, "Listen-

**Mode of transcendence -**

- A person who has knowledge of me, my activities and the workings of the illusory universe is transcendental;
- A person who desires salvation and wants to live with me in my divine abode is transcendental;
- A personal who believes that I am in all living beings me is transcendental;
- A person who has taken shelter of me is transcendental;
- A person who has faith in my devotional service is transcendental;
- Food that has been offered to me, before eating it, is transcendental;
- Happiness experienced due to association with me is transcendental.

**Remember this-** I am repeating this important fact often. You have received a human body. It's the proper vehicle to cultivate spiritual knowledge and its practical application.

Give up the association of the three material modes of nature and focus your attention on devotional service. After you are freed from the conditioning of the mind, as well as from the modes of nature, you will feel blissful by associating with me. You will no longer hanker for temporary, worldly pleasures."

# Deity Worship

Uddhava implored, "O Lord, I consider the worship of you in the deity form as the best and easy spiritual practice for all members of society. I know, for sure, you first gave instructions on deity worship to the gods. So, please describe the procedures for worshiping you as the deity in the temple. What qualifications must a devotee possess to worship you in this way, and what are the rules and regulations to be observed?"

Krishna smiled, "My dear Uddhava, I shall explain this subject to you briefly, from the beginning.

There are three methods for worshiping me- Vedic, Tantric, and mixed. A devotee should select the method that is best suited for him and then worship me according to the prescribed rules and regulations.

First, the devotee should clean his teeth and bathe. Then the devotee should perform the ritual known as *"anga nyasa"* (the process of purifying oneself by touching the various parts of the body while chanting *mantras*) on his own body.

After cleansing the body, the devotee should, then, concentrate his mind on me and chant the prescribed prayers, like the Gayatri Mantra, three times a day.

(https://en.wikipedia.org/wiki/Gayatri_Mantra)

This serves to purify the worshiper from his karmic burdens.

Let me now discuss the deity and its characteristics-

The deity form of the Lord can be made of eight different materials- precious stones, stone, wood, metal, earth, paint, sand or the mind. The deity can be established in two ways: permanent or temporary. If the devotee installs a permanent deity, it should never be removed from its place of installation or immersed in a body of water.

However, a temporary deity can be installed and then taken away. Remember this- the rituals for the permanent or temporary deities should always be performed when the deity is placed upon the ground.

The deity made of precious stones, stone or metal should be bathed with water.

If the deity is made of clay, paint, or wood then it should be cleaned thoroughly without using water.

One should worship the deity in the best manner possible. There are no rigid rules. A sincere devotee, who is free from material desires, can worship the deity with whatever is easily obtainable, or even within the mind. I do not accept even the most awesome offerings if they are given by nonbelievers, but I will readily accept even the most insignificant thing offered by a true devotee.

Of course, I appreciate it when the deity is decorated with beautiful clothes and ornaments and when fragrant oil, incense, flowers, and sattvic foods are offered to me with love.

After purifying himself and collecting all the paraphernalia for worship, the devotee should sit down on a mat of fresh, green grass, facing either east or north. If the deity is permanently installed, the worshiper should sit facing the deity. After cleansing the body (anga nyasa) the devotee should remove the remnants of previous offerings, such as flowers and flower garlands placed on the deity. He should then sprinkle water, kept in a clean vessel, on the place of worship, the paraphernalia for worship, and his own body. Next, he should decorate three vessels of water with sandalwood paste and flowers, which will be used for washing the deity's feet.

Next, the worshiper should purify the three vessels. He should sanctify the vessel holding water for washing the Lord's lotus feet by chanting *"hree-daya namah,"* the vessel containing water for oblation by chanting *"see-raa-say sva-ha,"* and the vessel containing water for washing the Lord's mouth by chanting *"see-kaa-yeh vasat."* The Gayatri Mantra should also be chanted for all three vessels.

Thereafter the devotee should meditate on my Lord Vishnu form, which is situated on the lotus of the heart, by vibrating the sacred syllable *"OM."* When my all pervasive divine form, is perceived by the worshiper, he should worship me internally, and then externally project me in the deity with full concentration. He should then perform nyasa on my divine body before beginning his worship.

The devotee should then mentally place a wooden, metal or stone seat that is sanctified. He should visualize my seat as an effulgent lotus flower with eight petals with saffron filaments within the whorl. Then, following the Vedic ritual traditions, he should place the deity on the seat and wash the deity's mouth, body and feet and offer oblations. By following this procedure, one enjoys material pleasures and attains salvation after death.

One should then worship, the Lord, his ornaments, weapons and associates of the Lord in their respective places, facing the altar from the eight directions. The Lord's vehicle "Garuda" should be worshipped in front of the altar and others in their specified places. The spiritual masters will be toward the left, and the demigods, headed by Indra, toward the east.

Depending upon the devotee's finances, he should bathe the deity daily with water mixed with sandalwood paste, camphor, kumkum powder etc.

While bathing the deity, he should recite the appropriate prayers.

After this, he should decorate the deity with fine clothing, ornaments, a sacred thread, the sacred dot/design on the forehead, a garland of flowers and basil leaves, sandalwood paste and fragrances.

If it is possible, the devotee should offer the deity sugar candy, sweet rice, ghee, rice-flour cakes, various sweet cakes, steamed rice-flour dumplings filled with sweet coconut and sugar, wheat cakes made with clarified butter and milk and covered with sugar and spices, yogurt, vegetable soups, and other palatable food. Do this only if you can afford it.

On special days, such as Ekadashi (the eleventh lunar day of the bright or dark fortnight of every lunar month) the deity should be smeared with fragrant oil, shown a mirror, offered a eucalyptus stick for brushing his teeth, bathed with the five kinds of nectar, offered varieties of opulent foods, and entertained with singing and dancing.

After constructing an arena and a raised altar, the devotee should perform a fire sacrifice.

He should ignite the sacrificial fire with wood that he has personally collected.

First, he should spread fresh green grass on the ground and sprinkle water over it. Then, he should place pieces of wood into the sacrificial fire while chanting the prescribed mantras. Thereafter, one should purify all of the items to be offered as oblations by sprinkling water upon them. After doing this, one should meditate upon the Lord as being situated within the sacrificial fire.

The intelligent devotee should thereafter meditate on the Lord and his divine features distinctly. Thereafter, the devotee should worship me by taking firewood soaked in clarified butter and placing it in the sacrificial fire.

He should then offer as oblations into the sacrificial fire various items soaked in clarified butter. He should then offer oblations to sixteen demigods, beginning with Yama, while reciting the mantras of each deity.

Having thus worshiped the Lord within the sacrificial fire, the devotee should offer his prayers and then worship the Lord's personal associates, headed by Nanda.

Next, the devotee should offer food to the Deity and then offer the remnants of the food offering to Visvaksena. He should, then, offer perfumed betel nuts to the Lord.

Thereafter, one should hear and chant the divine activities with true devotion and ponder over the divine messages in the stories. A devotee should always pray for the Lord's blessings, protection and salvation after death.

After praying in this way, the devotee should place the remnants of the flower garland (placed on the deity) upon his head. If the deity is temporary and is soon to be removed from its place of installation, the effulgence of the deity's presence should be withdrawn and placed within the lotus of one's heart.

Remember this- one should worship the Lord in the particular form that he has developed faith in. As the Supreme Soul of all, I exist within all created beings, as well as separately in my original form.

By worshiping me, as per established procedures, one achieves the state of perfection, both in this life and the next.

Devotees should construct a temple for their deity, along with flower gardens to provide flowers for the daily worship of the deity, as well as for festival occasions.

If a devotee offers the deity gifts of land, shops, towns, and villages, so that the regular worship and special festivals may continue in a grand manner, he will receive great material pleasures.

By installing the deity of the Lord, one becomes the ruler of the entire earth. By constructing a temple for the Lord, one becomes the ruler of the three worlds. By worshiping and serving the Deity, one attains residence in the heavenly planets, and by performing all three, one achieves a divine form like my own.

But one, who simply engages in devotional service without any desires or expectations, attains me. Thus, whoever worships me according to the process I have described will ultimately attain salvation.

If a person steals the property of the demigods or righteous persons, or assists, instigates, or simply approves of such an act, he will have to suffer as intestinal worms for ages.

The consequences will be directly proportionate to the degree of their participation.

That's it. I am done with my sermons. I hope, dear Uddhava, this knowledge made sense and you will start your journey of self-realization."

## Uddhava Bids Farewell to the Lord

After listening to Lord Krishna, Uddhava was awestruck by the universal truths. He bowed down to touch the Lord's feet with his head, as a sign of reverence, and then spoke with folded hands.

Uddhava prayed, "O Divine Lord, My entire life was spent in the darkness of ignorance but by your divine sermons, my delusions about the material world have gone.

I am standing in the sunlight of knowledge. Now, no cold, darkness, fear or even death can ever torment me. I am eternally grateful to you, Lord, for illuminating me with transcendental knowledge.

Please advise me what I need to do from here."

Krishna advised, "My dearest Uddhava, go to **Badrikashrama**. Bathe in the sacred **Alakananda** River. Wear tree bark and eat the fruit and roots of the forest.

Contemplate over what I talked about and assimilate their essence. Be self-satisfied, desireless, self-controlled, peaceful, and soaked with transcendental knowledge and self-realization.

Focus your total attention upon me, and in this way, you will not be affected by the three modes of material nature. You finally come back to me and enjoy eternal bliss."

Uddhava though self-realized could not bear to leave the Lord. He was tear-stricken with grief. However, the Lord's instructions had to be obeyed. He said a final goodbye and departed.

Thereafter, Uddhava went to Badrikashrama and practiced the yoga meditation taught by the Lord. By engaging in constant meditation, he attained the Lord's eternal abode, Vaikuntha.

## Lord Krishna Ascends to Vaikuntha

After the annihilation of the Yadavas, Lord Krishna had to fulfill a curse given to him by **Gandhari**, his great devotee and the mother of the Kauravas.

### What's this curse about?

It all started with the dynastic struggle between two groups of paternal first cousins of an Indo-Aryan clan, **Kuru**. The two groups, the **Kauravas** and the **Pandavas**, are in constant conflict with each other for the throne of **Hastinapura**.

The five sons of the deceased **King Pandu** are the Pandavas and the one hundred sons (and one daughter) of the blind **King Dhritarashtra**, the Kauravas. Although the Kauravas are the senior branch of the family, **Duryodhana**, the eldest Kaurava, is younger than **Yudhisthira**, the eldest Pandava. Both Duryodhana and Yudhisthira claim to be first in line to inherit the throne.

The conflict between the Kauravas and the Pandavas culminates in the great battle of **Kurukshetra** (Kuru's field). Vast armies from all over the Indian (**Bharat**) subcontinent fought alongside the two rivals. In the end, the Pandavas, with Lord Krishna's help, kill the Kauravas and their allies, and emerge victorious in the eighteen day war.

After the battle, Lord Krishna visited Gandhari to offer his condolences. In a fit of rage and sorrow, Gandhari cursed Krishna that just as the Kuru dynasty had ended fighting with each other, likewise, after thirty years, the Yadava clan would end fighting and killing each other. Gandhari felt that Lord Krishna was responsible for all the bloodshed. She cursed that Krishna would also die a disgusting death in the forest just like her eldest son, **Duryodhana** had.

Lord Krishna happily accepted the curse.

Thirty years ago, Gandhari had cursed Krishna. The time had come for the curse to take effect. He went to the forest and sat under the **peepal** (**Ficus Religiosa**) tree, placing his left foot, which looked like a red lily, on his right thigh.

A hunter named **Jara,** who happened to be around, mistook the left foot as a deer's mouth and shot his arrow at it. He immediately discovered his blunder and fell at the Lord's feet and begged for forgiveness.

Jara cried out, "O Lord Krishna, what a sinner I am to have struck you! Please forgive me for this grave sin. It was an honest mistake on my part. I mistook your foot for a deer and shot at it. Please kill me so that I will never hurt or kill innocent beings again."

Krishna consoled, "Hey, Jara, get up. It was not your fault. You shot at me as per my divine will. Your reward will be a place by my side at Vaikuntha. Behold the aerial vehicle that is coming to take you to my heavenly abode."

**What happened next?**

Jara circumambulated the Lord thrice and entered the aerial vehicle which landed near him. The ship rose up in the sky and disappeared from view.

**Daruka**, Lord Krishna's charioteer came to the forest in search of his master. He smelled the divine fragrance and followed it. He saw the Lord leaning against the tree with an arrow piercing his toe. He sensed that the Lord was about to leave the world and he was tear stricken. The Lord consoled him and ordered him to go to Dwaraka, in quick haste, and take the surviving family members to the Pandavas' kingdom, **Hastinapura**. Daruka bowed with tear-filled eyes and left immediately to comply with the Lord's wishes.

Lord Brahma, Lord Shiva, their wives, the demigods and other celestial beings, sensing that Lord Krishna was about to leave the earth for Vaikuntha, hovered around the peepal tree. They chanted prayers and showered flowers over the Lord.

The Lord looked up and blessed the extra-terrestrials. He, then, closed his eyes as if he was in yogic meditation.

**In the blink of an eye, the Supreme Being ascended to Vaikuntha.**

**The End**

## Thank You!

Thank you for reading my book. If you enjoyed it, it would be greatly appreciated if you left a review so others can receive the same benefits you have. Your review will help me see what is and isn't working so I can better serve you and all my other readers even more.

Here's the link

**https://www.amazon.com/dp/B01FV75BZK**
**http://ASIN.cc/2RBb5kL**

Please visit my Amazon Author Page

http://Author.to/MikeNach

Thanks again for your support!

# My Other Books!

If you liked this book, you will like these too:

## Eastern Religions:

**Game of Illusions: Ashtavakra Gita**

http://ASIN.cc/ytWryA

**Game of Life: New Age Bhagavad Gita**

http://ASIN.cc/1Q7_D9W

**The Final Teachings of Lord Krishna spoke, " Uddhava Gita**

http://ASIN.cc/1ib2Sqf

## Christianity:

**The Secret Gospel of Thomas: Decoded**

http://ASIN.cc/1Y9SQ8W

**How to Be Enriched in Every Way**

http://ASIN.cc/12Jo4zL

**Betrayer or the Chosen One? Judas Tells His Side**

http://ASIN.cc/1ZePUvf

**I Have Sinned: The Judas Chronicles**

http://ASIN.cc/26P4oxf

Occult and Magick:

**HOW TO BE THE MASTER OF THE UNIVERSE**

http://ASIN.cc/ychKfq

**HOW TO GET ANYTHING YOU WANT? MAKE A MAGICK MIRROR!**

http://ASIN.cc/RahVJf

**How to Be the Master of Mystic Yoga**
http://ASIN.cc/2BnNYZW

Investing:

**HOW TO BE THE MASTER OF THE STOCK MARKET**

http://ASIN.cc/2QV4XQL

**I CHING OF THE STOCK MARKET**

http://ASIN.cc/bxxqcL

**THE 40 PARABLES OF INVESTING**

http://ASIN.cc/11ujpiL

**30 Essential Rules for New Investors**

http://ASIN.cc/1fAN0Rf

Fiction:

## WHY ME? Abridged Version

http://ASIN.cc/e5qS5f

## WHY ME? The Complete and Uncut Edition

http://ASIN.cc/22nkGcf

### Advice:

## THE HARE AND THE TORTOISE -BEAT THE BULLIES!

http://ASIN.cc/mocBz0

## The Little Book That Beats the Bullies

http://ASIN.cc/12QD6kW

## DATING ADVICE: 30 Frequently Asked Questions

http://ASIN.cc/V_YBvf

Printed in Great Britain
by Amazon